THE PROTEUS PARADOX

NICK

YEE

THE

PROTEUS

PARADOX

HOW ONLINE

GAMES AND

VIRTUAL WORLDS

CHANGE US—

AND HOW THEY

DON'T

Yale
UNIVERSITY
PRESS

NEW HAVEN &
LONDON

Yale University Press books may be purchased in quantity for educational, business, or promotional use. For information, please e-mail sales.press@yale.edu (US office) or sales@yaleup.co.uk (UK office).

Set in Monotype Joanna type by Keystone Typesetting, Inc., Orwigsburg, Pennsylvania.

Printed in the United States of America.

Library of Congress Cataloging-in-Publication Data

Yee, Nick, 1979–
The proteus paradox : how online games and virtual worlds change us—
and how they don't / Nick Yee.
   p.   cm.
Includes bibliographical references and index.
ISBN 978-0-300-19099-1 (hardback)
1. Computer games. 2. Virtual reality. 3. Shared virtual environments. I. Title.
GV1469.15.Y44 2014
794.8—dc23   2013024662

A catalogue record for this book is available from the British Library.

This paper meets the requirements of ANSI/NISO Z39.48–1992 (Permanence of Paper).

10 9 8 7 6 5 4 3 2 1

To Doug, for showing me that this was possible

CONTENTS

ACKNOWLEDGMENTS

Throughout my research career, I've been incredibly fortunate to have had supportive and prescient mentors who helped me think about and study online games and virtual worlds in new ways. At Haverford College in 1998, Doug Davis's course on personality psychology also involved learning how to hand code HTML and run web surveys. When I proposed an independent study project exploring *EverQuest* gamers, Doug unknowingly launched my research career by helping me identify the psychological questions waiting to be answered. His ideas of how psychology and technology intersect have always been and remain an inspiration. During my graduate program at Stanford University, Jeremy Bailenson's contagious intensity and drive led to the four most productive years of my academic career as we used virtual reality to understand what it means to have a digital avatar. I couldn't have asked for a more supportive and astute graduate adviser who could discuss theory, methods, and technical tools with the same savviness. It was also during my graduate program when Nic Ducheneaut brought me onboard as an intern at the Palo Alto Research Center as he pioneered new ways of collecting and analyzing large-scale data in online games. As a mentor and colleague over the past eight years, we've shared some amazing adventures together in game data. This book would not be possible without them.

Over the past decade, more than fifty-five thousand online gamers have participated in my surveys. I cannot thank them enough for their time, their willingness to share their stories, and their insightful comments.

At LaunchBooks, my agent, David Fugate, helped me understand the publishing world and figure out what kind of book I wanted to write. And last but not least, Joe Calamia at Yale University Press tirelessly read and reread drafts and revisions, always providing insightful suggestions on how to improve the flow, the structure, and the prose. I'd like to thank him for all his help throughout the proposal and writing process, and for making this a better book.

THE PROTEUS PARADOX

I needed to create a mirror. I was a graduate student at Stanford University, and several undergraduates with graphics and programming backgrounds were helping me build a virtual room for a research study. Our initial idea would have required complicated trigonometric calculations based on the viewer's head position and what part of the room was visible behind him or her. The director of the Virtual Human Interaction Lab, Jeremy Bailenson, helped us cross this technical hurdle. Instead of using a reflective mirror, he suggested making a hole in the virtual room's wall. Through this hole, the viewer would see an adjoining, flipped replica of the room. And a digital doppelgänger in that flipped room would mimic the viewer's every movement. Virtual cloning triumphed over trigonometry, but we still had a problem: it was all too perfect. Instead of acting like a mirror, it looked like a stranger staring at you and mocking your movements from another room. With only a few days left before the study began, I had an idea. I added a translucent sheet of water stains in front of our mirror. With some grime, our mirror came together. Even in a virtual world, imperfection proved more believable.

In the lab experiment itself, we gave participants either an attractive or an unattractive avatar. They would see their new virtual selves in the virtual mirror and then interact with a virtual stranger. Within sixty seconds of being given a new digital body, participants in attractive avatars became friendlier and shared more personal information with the stranger than participants in unattractive avatars. Changing avatar height had a similar effect: people given taller avatars became more confident than people given shorter ones. Crucially, these behavioral changes followed users even when they had left the virtual world. Those recently given attractive avatars selected more attractive partners in a separate offline task. As we create and endlessly customize our avatars, they in turn influence how we think and how we behave. Virtual worlds change and control us in unexpected ways.

Bailenson and I coined a term for this power of avatars: the Proteus Effect. In the *Odyssey*, Homer describes the sea god Proteus as being able to change his physical form at will:

> First he turned into a great bearded lion,
> and then to a serpent, then to a leopard, then to a great boar,
> and he turned into fluid water, to a tree with towering branches.[1]

Proteus encapsulates one of the promises of virtual worlds: the ability to reinvent ourselves, to be one and many at the same time. But in my research, I have cataloged the inadvertent ways in which virtual worlds control how we think and behave. And more often than not, these behavioral changes have unlikely sources—things that we wouldn't have expected to have power over us, such as our avatars' height or whether we can ask a preprogrammed city guard for directions when we're lost.

Every day, millions of people log into massively multiplayer online role-playing games (often referred to as MMORPGs or just MMOs), like *World of Warcraft* or *EverQuest*, and interact with each other via fantasy characters of their own creation. These online games allow people from all over the world to embark on adventures together, exploring dark dungeons and finding magical treasures. At its peak, *World of Warcraft* had twelve million subscribers. In 2012, an estimated twenty million users had active monthly subscriptions to online games, the most common way of playing online games in North America and Europe. In Asia, online games use a free-to-play model instead of requiring monthly subscriptions and derive profit instead from selling premium items or services within the game. In China, at least two online games have recorded a peak concurrent usage of over two million gamers—*Fantasy Westward Journey* and *Zheng Tu Online*. And online games were expected to generate $6.1 billion in China alone in 2012. Virtual worlds designed specifically for kids have also done well in recent years. The free-to-play game *Club Penguin*, for example, had seven hundred thousand paying subscribers in 2007 when Disney purchased the company for $350 million.[2]

At first glance, these fantasy worlds could not be more detached from reality—after all, gnomes and dragons belong in storybooks. And indeed, when online games burst into the public consciousness in the early to mid-2000s, the media portrayed them as a seductive escape. In a 2006 article in the *Washington Post*, "Lost in an Online Fantasy World," Olga Kazan noted that online gamers "can be sorcerers or space pilots, their identities woven into a world so captivating, it is too incredible to ever leave. Unfortunately, some of them don't." A piece published the same year in the *San Francisco Chronicle* went further: "The Internet once was seen as a golden information superhighway transporting the next generation to the Promised Land. Now it may feel more like a minefield—seductive on the surface, but seeded with subterranean hazards." Even when academics challenged the presumed dangers of online games, the counterargument was often still rooted in escapism. In his book *Synthetic Worlds*, economist Edward Castronova countered that escaping into virtual worlds is actually a positive and rational decision for some players: "And for those for whom Real Life: The Game is indeed joyless, the synthetic world evidently represents a game that has many of the same features but is more fun to play. Its use therefore represents a choice, a completely rationale one in fact."[3]

Many researchers have emphasized the hopeful promises of freedom and empowerment in virtual worlds and online games. In her 1995 book on textual virtual worlds, ethnographer and psychologist Sherry Turkle wrote that these new worlds "encourage us to think of ourselves as fluid, emergent, decentralized, multiplicitous, flexible, and ever in progress." Though Turkle's current work is more pessimistic, recent books on gaming argue even more strongly for similar potentials. Game designer Jane McGonigal's 2011 book *Reality Is Broken* has the tagline, "Why games make us better and how they can change the world," and argues that games can powerfully contribute to happiness and improve the quality of our lives. And anthropologist Bonnie Nardi wrote that online games allow "a release of creativity and a sense of empowerment in conditions of autonomy, sociality, and positive reward."[4]

I am not as optimistic. Instead of an escape from the drudgeries of the physical world, many online gamers describe their gameplay as an unpaid second job. And instead of freedom and empowerment in online games, I found quite the opposite: superstitious behaviors such as ritual dances pervade online games; a gamer's offline nationality can be a matter of virtual life and death; and false gender stereotypes are being made true when we play online games. Even when we believe we are free and empowered, our offline politics and cognitive baggage prevent us from changing. And where we think we are fully in control, unique psychological levers in virtual worlds (such as our avatars) powerfully change how we think and behave. This is the Proteus Paradox. Without a more careful look how these spaces do and do not change us, the promises of virtual worlds and online games are being subverted.

Video gamers no longer form a fringe subculture; these games are rapidly converging with many aspects of our everyday lives. Not only are millions of people spending on average twenty hours per week in these online games, business corporations are increasingly exploring how the psychological principles from gaming can be harnessed for corporate work. The consulting company Gartner has predicted that by 2014, 70 percent of Global 2000 companies will have at least one application that incorporates gaming mechanisms. Games are also where people have started to form long-term relationships. Ten percent of online gamers have physically dated someone they first met in a virtual world. Games are becoming an integral part of our lives— they are where we play, where we work, and where we fall in love. But technology isn't a neutral tool that simply bends to our will. When we adopt new gadgets, those gadgets help shape how we think, behave, and interact with one another. As millions of people spend increasing amounts of time in online games and virtual worlds, we need to be vigilant about whether these new environments are fulfilling their promises of freedom and reinvention, and if they're not, we need to find a way to change them.

The first part of the book provides an introduction to online games and dispels some myths about who plays. In the second part, I focus on different aspects of online games that challenge their promises of freedom and escape. We'll look at superstitions, stereotypes, the work of dragon-slaying, and falling in love. And in the final part, I move from an explanation of how virtual worlds don't change us to describing the unexpected ways that they do. In this section, I describe how virtual worlds come with a unique set of psychological tools—whether it's our avatars or the rules of death—that can modify our attitudes and behaviors. I end the book with my thoughts on the possible trajectories of virtual worlds and what it might take to change our current course.

Many of this book's findings come from web survey data from more than fifty thousand online gamers. The questions I asked ranged from basic demographics to gameplay motivations, from how players fell in love to how they picked the names for their characters. I ran new surveys every few months, and thousands of players would respond over a weekend. Findings would fuel new questions and directions. I often started exploring a topic with open-ended questions—"Tell me how you fell in love in the game"—and once I got a handle on the range of responses, I would use more focused, multiple-choice questions to gather quantitative data. The Internet also gave me a way to share my research findings and engage with gamers. I created a research blog, the Daedalus Project (I have a penchant for names from Greek mythology), that cataloged the survey results and publicized new surveys. The project was active from 2003 to 2009. In this book, I share many player stories from the Daedalus Project, allowing players' own voices to explain why these online games are so engaging and unforgettable. To improve the readability of these narratives, I have expanded all acronyms of game titles and corrected minor typos. At the end of each player quotation, I include the game that player was actively playing when they took the survey. Thus, players with multiple online gaming careers may mention a game title in their response other than the one explicitly noted. In the latter part of the book, I also present my findings from lab studies and large-scale data analysis of in-game data. I describe these projects in detail separately when they are introduced.[5]

I wrote this book with a diverse audience in mind, presuming expertise in neither online gaming nor the social sciences but with an eye toward highlighting the many intersections between these two areas. We'll see how one psychologist's experiments with pigeons help us understand superstitions in online games and ask why we need virtual chairs if our virtual bodies never get tired. Rather than focusing on abstract theory or gamer jargon, this book leverages provocative findings from a wide range of data sources: player narratives and statistics from online surveys, results from psychology experiments, and analysis of in-game data logs. Whether it's gnomes in love or the consequences of virtual death, each chapter delves into a different aspect of online gaming to help readers understand what these virtual worlds are about and why they matter. For readers who are unfamiliar with online games, a glossary of online gaming terms is provided at the end of the book.

Gamers already familiar with online games will learn about the many psychological mechanisms that influence their behavior in games: why superstitions are so pervasive or how your avatar can change the way you interact with other people. They will also learn the many statistics of gameplay behavior documented, such as the percentage of men and women who gender-bend—inhabiting an avatar of the opposite gender. Nongaming parents and spouses of gamers will find a guided cultural tour of online games addressing who plays these games, whether gaming addiction is real, and what collaboration and love mean in these virtual worlds. And game designers and analysts will understand why gamers don't always play by the rules—for example, creating their own in the case of superstitions, and how to process and make sense of the wealth of data available in their game logs.

This book is about more than games. It questions what it means to be human in a digital world and how technology changes who we are, how we live, and how we form relationships.

CHAPTER 1 THE NEW WORLD

A good way to understand online games is to trace how they emerged from the intersection of several historical trajectories: miniature wargaming, epic fantasy literature, role-playing games, and multiplayer video games. In 1812, the Prussian army developed *Kriegsspiel*, a complex tabletop board game, to train officers in military tactics and strategy. It was certainly not the first board game about war—chess also fits the description—but where chess is a metaphorical abstraction, the Prussians developed *Kriegsspiel* to be a realistic war simulation. Miniature figures represented infantry and cavalry armies; square terrain tiles, laid out on the table, created a grid-based map; and dice determined individual combat outcomes. Rules governed how far each unit could move each turn, how much damage each unit could inflict, and how terrain modified movement and combat. A neutral umpire would assess and resolve the players' actions. In the 1880s, the United States imported *Kriegspiel*, again for military training purposes. Miniature wargames first became commercially available in 1913, when the writer H. G. Wells simplified the rules, added a mechanical cannon, and sold the toy soldier package as *Little Wars*.[1]

In addition to simulating contemporary warfare, miniature wargaming branched into other time periods, such as the medieval era. In 1968, Gary Gygax developed a medieval wargaming ruleset for his local gaming group. He extended an existing ruleset and added such features as jousting and one-on-one duels. As he later said in an interview,

> Not long after that, as the members began to get tired of medieval games, and I wasn't, I decided to add fantasy elements to the mix, such as a dragon that had a fire-breath weapon, a "hero" that was worth four normal warriors, a wizard who could cast fireballs (the range and hit diameter of a large catapult) and lightning bolts (the range and hit area of a cannon), and so forth. I converted a plastic stegosaurus into a pretty fair dragon, as there were no models of them around in those days.

This new game, published and sold in 1972 as Chainmail, was novel for two reasons. First, it shifted the focus from army squadrons to individuals. Players no longer controlled an army; they controlled one character, a heroic figure. And second, the game retained combat realism but moved away from modeling physical reality and historical warfare. Dragons were now fair game.[2]

Of course, these fantasy elements were popular with Gygax's wargaming group in the late 1960s largely because of J. R. R. Tolkien's Lord of the Rings trilogy, published in Britain between 1954 and 1955 and in the United States in 1966. Fantasy creatures had existed in literature long before Tolkien, but The Lord of the Rings wasn't simply a story with fantasy creatures; it was an epic fantasy with unique races, centuries of fascinating history, and a varied set of political factions vying for power. Tolkien didn't merely write about characters; he created a parallel world. In a sense, Gygax's Chainmail was an initial answer to the hypothetical question: What if you wanted to be a heroic character in Middle Earth rather than just reading about Legolas, Gimli, or Aragorn in a book?

Shortly after *Chainmail*, Gygax began working with game designer Dave Arneson to develop a more elaborate and self-contained ruleset because *Chainmail*, though popular among wargaming enthusiasts, assumed extensive prior knowledge of wargaming conventions. This new ruleset shifted the focus of battle location from outdoor terrain to monster-infested dungeons. The resulting stand-alone game, published in 1974, was *Dungeons and Dragons*. It created a new gaming genre: role-playing games. The popularity of Tolkien's epic fantasy left a clear mark on this new game genre. As Gygax put it, "Just about all the players were huge JRRT [Tolkien] fans, and so they insisted that I put as much Tolkien-influence material into the game as possible. Anyone reading this that recalls the original D&D game will know that there were Balrogs, Ents, and Hobbits in it." At the same time, he has stated that Tolkien was only one of many sources of inspiration. Thus, *Dungeons and Dragons* clearly borrowed Hobbits and Ents from Tolkien, but the game also welcomed Medusa and vampires from Greek mythology and medieval lore.[3]

In role-playing games, players first create their characters based on predefined templates of different races and abilities in the rulebook. Elves may be more proficient in archery, and Dwarves may be able to endure more combat damage before dying. Players can choose from different combat specializations, such as warriors trained for combat or mages trained for casting spells. Combat is initiated and won using conventions from miniature wargames. A two-handed sword may inflict "2d6" damage—"2d6" refers to rolling two six-sided dice and taking the total, thus inflicting between 2 and 12 damage points. Characters and monsters have health points, and when the combat damage exceeds their health points, they die. As characters defeat monsters, they accumulate experience points and ascend to higher levels. This allows them to improve on skills or learn new ones over time. Typical role-playing campaigns are weekly social gatherings that may run weeks, months, or even years. One frustrating feature of role-playing games is the constant need to reference tables in the rulesets. There are tables that list the damage of every weapon, tables for each monster's health points, tables for how skills improve as characters level up, and tables for suitable treasure for different character levels. Almost every rule in the game has an accompanying reference table. As role-playing games became more complex, the computerized automation of dice-rolling and referencing tables was a natural progression.

Online games emerged in the media and the public consciousness around the turn of the millennium, but networked computer games existed as early as 1969. The University of Illinois, funded by the National Science Foundation, created an experimental computer-based teaching system. Named PLATO, for Programmed Logic for Automated Teaching Operations, the system consisted of a set of computer terminals connected to a central mainframe computer. The terminals were "dumb" in the sense that as simple input and output devices they merely relayed information to and from the mainframe, which carried out all the computation. A programming language allowed users to create programs, and thus games, of their own. In 1969, Rick Blomme used PLATO to program *Spacewar*, a game in which two players controlled their own spaceships and attacked each other. The graphics consisted of a monochrome, top-down view of the star field. PLATO's terminals were located all over the campus, and this meant that two users could play against each other remotely, making *Spacewar* a networked game. The first three-dimensional, networked, multiplayer computer game, *Maze War*, appeared in 1974. In this game, eyeball avatars represented players who would chase and shoot each other in a maze. The monochrome line-based graphics provided a first-person perspective of the maze.[4]

Maze War paved the way for action shooter games like *Quake* and *Doom*. The predecessor for computer-based role-playing games came a few years later. In 1976, Will Crowther created ADVENT, a single-player text-based adventure game that led to games such as *Zork*. ADVENT plays like a fantasy-infused dungeon explorer, inspired by Crowther's experience with *Dungeons and Dragons* and his interest in cave exploration. The game begins with the following text: "You are standing at the end of a road before a small brick building. Around you is a forest. A small stream flows out of the building and down a gully." Players moved around and performed actions by typing in keywords. For example, if a player typed "go in," he or she would see the following text:

> You are inside a building, a well house for a large spring.
> There are some keys on the ground here.
> There is a shiny brass lamp nearby.
> There is food here.

There were also fantasy elements in ADVENT, such as a bridge guarded by a troll who demanded payment for crossing.[5]

It wasn't long before someone figured out how to create a multi-user adventure game. In 1978, Roy Trubshaw, a student at Essex University, began developing a multiuser version of DUNGEN, a text-based adventure game inspired by ADVENT. The very first version of MUD (Multi-User Dungeon), still text-based, was released in the fall of 1978. Richard Bartle, a fellow student, soon joined Trubshaw in developing MUD: "The game was originally little more than a series of inter-connected locations where you could move and chat. . . . Roy was mainly interested in the programming side of things, rather than the design of rooms, puzzles and so on. When he left Essex, I took over full control. At that point, there was no objective for the players, and only primitive communication." Drawing from his interest in board games, Bartle added many game elements to MUD, such as a combat system, an experience system that permitted characters to level up, and puzzles. In 1980, Essex University's computer network was connected to ARPANet, the network that became the Internet, and this meant that MUD became a full-fledged Internet-based game.[6]

The separate historical threads we've been following so far—miniature wargaming, epic fantasy literature, role-playing games, and multiplayer video games—finally intersected with the creation of MUD. As with ADVENT, other developers began creating variants of the original MUD, changing the game design and adapting the code to different computer systems. These variants in turn started their own lineages of MUD code bases; among them were TinyMUDs, AberMUDs, and DikuMUDs. In the 1980s, MUDs began to appear on commercial online services such as America Online (AOL) and CompuServe. One notable MUD was *Island of Kesmai*, the first online role-playing game to display rudimentary graphics using ASCII symbols—mazes and rooms, for example, were created using dash, pipe, and asterisk characters on the screen. MUDs were cash cows for these early Internet service providers because users paid for each hour spent online. *Island of Kesmai* cost six dollars per hour on 300-baud modems and twelve dollars per hour on 1200-baud modems. This meant that early online games could be very profitable even with relatively small player bases, as long as there were enough dedicated players. The first multiplayer online role-playing game to display true graphics—that is, using colored pixels to represent characters and the virtual world—was *NeverWinter Nights*, launched on AOL in 1991. The game used graphics to render the world and the characters in a top-down 2D representation. The game server's initial capacity of two hundred concurrent players was eventually upgraded to five hundred concurrent players.[7]

Early online games required much of both developers and consumers. Good graphical capabilities were not standard on personal computers in the early 1990s, and Internet connection fees via the early service providers were pricy. On the development side, the creation of online games required teams with incredibly broad skill sets; these teams needed to pioneer methods for rendering 3D graphics, create server technology that could handle thousands of concurrent users, and figure out how to manage online communities in which players could stalk, harass, and kill each other. It was 1996 when *Meridian 59*, the first 3D massively multiplayer online game, launched. Players could now see the game world rendered in three-dimensional graphics from a first-person perspective. Instead of having to play the game through AOL or CompuServe, anyone with an Internet connection could join. *Meridian 59* also has the distinction of being the first online game to employ a monthly subscription model. The game charged players ten dollars per month, regardless of how many hours they played.[8]

Although many recognize *Meridian 59* as the first 3D massively multiplayer online role-playing game, this unwieldy label actually wasn't coined until a year later, in 1997, by Richard Garriott, the producer of *Ultima Online*. Before this, many gamers referred to these games as graphical MUDs. What constitutes "massively" has never been standardized: Is it the number of total active players or the highest number of concurrent players or the greatest possible number of players a server can handle? Perhaps the best way to understand "massively" is that it differentiated the genre from other multi-player online games available in that era. For example, multiplayer shooter games like *Quake* could handle up to sixteen concurrent players on each server. This means that there is some wiggle room as to which game can claim to be the first in the genre. After all, in 1991 *NeverWinter Nights* could handle five hundred concurrent users.

Ultima Online's highly successful launch in 1997 changed the playing field, and the game eventually peaked with roughly 250,000 active subscribers. *Ultima Online* made it clear that the industry was no longer looking at a niche gaming subgenre that catered to a handful of hardcore players. *EverQuest*'s launch in 1999 was an even larger commercial success, with an eventual peak of 450,000 players. With the shift to subscription-based revenues, the number of total active players mattered more than the number of hardcore players. It also meant that a retail game continued to generate revenue month after month after its purchase. Game companies were quick to realize the significant commercial potential of this model. *Ultima Online* and *Ever-Quest* are often recognized as popularizing this game genre and bringing online games into the public consciousness.[9]

The success of *Ultima Online* and *EverQuest* led to a surge of online games in the following years. Games such as *Asheron's Call* and *Dark Age of Camelot* stayed within the medieval fantasy setting. Others, such as *EVE Online* and *Star Wars Galaxies*, took the gameplay mechanisms to futuristic settings. The success of the genre among older teenagers and adults led to the development of virtual worlds for preteens in games like *Habbo Hotel*, *Club Penguin*, and *Toontown Online*. Despite the large number of online games launched during this time, there was a general consensus in the game industry by 2004 that the online game player base had reached a plateau; new games would simply siphon players from older games. No online game in the American or European markets had approached the million subscriber mark, and the overall number of players did not seem to be growing. Yet that year Blizzard launched *World of Warcraft*. Within months, the game had a million players. In early 2006, when the game broke the six million subscriber mark, Blizzard announced that it had more than a million subscribers in Europe—four times higher than the previously estimated size of the entire European market for online games. As of the writing of this book in 2013, no other online game in the US or European market has come close to matching *World of Warcraft*'s peak player base of twelve million paying subscribers. This is remarkable, given that it has been eight years since the game launched.[10]

One Short Day

Even though online games can have wildly different settings—ranging from medieval fantasy to intergalactic science fiction to contemporary cityscapes—their core gameplay is remarkably similar. Contemporary online games draw heavily from the conventions of miniature wargaming and tabletop role-playing games. Players begin all online games by creating their character, a weak novice who slowly gains experience and becomes more powerful. Players can select from a range of *races* (such as Elf, Troll, or Human) and *classes* (such as Warrior, Mage, or Cleric), each with unique strengths and weaknesses. Depending on the game, players can customize the appearance of their character by selecting different hairstyles, skin tones, and clothing.

The core gameplay revolves around leveling up the character. When players kill a monster, their character gains experience and an assortment of gold coins and equipment from the slain creature; this assortment is collectively called *loot* in gamer jargon. When a character has gained sufficient experience, that character levels up and either learns new abilities or improves its existing abilities. In broad strokes, these games are about killing monsters and selling loot to buy bigger swords to kill even bigger monsters that drop more valuable loot. In online games, players refer to monsters as *mobs*, short for "mobiles," a term coined by Bartle in the original MUD.[11]

These games encourage players to cooperate in a variety of ways. Although it is often possible to fight creatures and level up alone, this generally becomes more difficult beyond the beginner areas. Also, different character classes complement one another well when taking on more challenging monsters. There is a "holy trinity" in terms of combat class synergy that is important to understand. In a group encounter with hostile monsters, heavily armored *tank* classes shield the group from enemy attacks while lightly armored *DPS* (high Damage Per Second) classes inflict large amounts of damage from a distance. *Healer* classes restore health lost during combat to prevent their team members from dying. All gameplay tactics and strategies derive from these three class archetypes. Tanks need to make sure they vigilantly taunt and distract monsters, known as maintaining *aggro*—short for aggression. DPS need to maximize damage output without drawing aggro. And healers need to selectively heal their group while preserving their *mana*—a resource used to cast spells that regenerates slowly. Typical group encounters take place in dungeons, and challenging end-game encounters with boss monsters are usually termed *raids*.

Because of the number of players needed to conduct a raid (up to twenty-five players in *World of Warcraft*), players form large, persistent social groups known as *guilds*. Guild founders create a unique name for their guild (for example, The Druid Circle), take on a leadership role, and delegate officer roles as the guild grows. In these games, players communicate via typed chat. Newer games provide voice tools that allow players to chat directly using headsets with microphones. Online games typically also provide a set of virtual "emotes" that have visual animations. For example, typing "/dance" causes your character to loop through a dance animation. And in addition to combat skills, many online games allow players to learn and level up in noncombat abilities, such as tailoring, blacksmithing, and alchemy.

Most online games provide different game servers with slightly different rules that cater to different players. For example, there are usually servers on which players are able to kill each other. This activity is usually referred to as player-versus-player, or PvP. Servers on which this is not allowed are marked player-versus-environment, or PvE. Even on PvE servers in many games, consenting players can kill each other in certain situations. In *World of Warcraft*, for example, players can choose to enter into battlegrounds or to initiate duels.

Historical Accidents and Digital Vestiges

Hindsight streamlines history, often inaccurately. Many gamers think that MUD descended directly from *Dungeons and Dragons*, but according to Bartle, the "Dungeon" in MUD "has nothing to do with the role-playing game Dungeons and Dragons." As I noted earlier, it derived instead from Trubshaw's interest in the adventure game DUNGEN. In fact, some later MUDs tried more explicitly to replicate the game mechanisms of *Dungeons and Dragons*. For example, developers in the department of computer science at the University of Copenhagen created DikuMUD in 1990 specifically to capture more of the *Dungeons and Dragons* spirit—twelve years after the creation of the original MUD. The evolution of online games didn't follow a linear genealogy so much as it repeatedly and spontaneously coalesced in a shared cultural consciousness in which Tolkien, role-playing games, and networked computing were popular. Raph Koster, the lead designer of *Ultima Online*, has said that "MMOs were created simultaneously and independently by a dozen groups at once. The folks doing Meridian 59 did not know about the folks doing Kingdom of the Winds, and so on. Not to mention older antecedents like Habitat. MUDs, in fact, were also invented independently at least four times." Of course, this is not to say that online games emerged the same way every time. In discussing the history of role-playing games and MUDs, Bartle has said, "Dungeons and Dragons was a seed, which, when it planted, grew in a particular way. And if it had been planted in, say, another country or at another time, it would have grown differently." Online games may have been inevitable, but the online games available are influenced by historical factors. The large budgets needed to develop online games increase risk adversity and encourage copying the formulas of successful games, and certain archetypes become deeply entrenched within the industry. As Koster has noted, "MMOs have removed more features from MUD gameplay than they have added, when you look at the games in aggregate."[12]

Online games like *World of Warcraft* are the primary implementations of virtual worlds we have right now; there are no other three-dimensional, persistent virtual worlds that rival their use—whether in terms of active users or amount of time spent in them. Because of how similar these online games have become, we've largely stopped asking how they can be any different. On game forums, players tend to ask for improvements of existing features—larger-scale group conflicts or deeper character specialization. But online games as we know them are a very idiosyncratic implementation of virtual worlds; there is nothing preordained about this historical accident. One of these idiosyncrasies is the focus on small group combat. It's true that the metaphor of war is pervasive across video games, but it's telling that the first massively multiplayer online role-playing game was launched in 1996, yet SimCity, the popular city-building game franchise, introduced large-scale multiplayer features only in 2013.[13]

These idiosyncratic vestiges in online games affect how they influence us. The emphasis on combat in these games stems from their wargaming roots. In chapter 4, I describe how this ancestry comes full circle in high-level guilds that focus on raiding; many of these guilds adopt militaristic hierarchies and require strict obedience and discipline from their members. The reliance on deeply numerical gameplay also stems from wargaming conventions. Fantasy and math aren't natural bedfellows, but the complex rulesets and tables of wargaming brought this unlikely pair together. In chapter 3, I explain how the complex mathematical outcomes in online games play into our brain's eagerness to make sense of the world, leading to the emergence of superstitions. It is also this numerical system that makes it so easy to collect, quantify, and analyze data from online games—free-form storytelling would be much harder to process and analyze. In chapter 9, we'll see how these accessible data sets can be used to infer a player's gender or even personality. And finally, Gygax's shift to individual combat in Chainmail is why we play online games with an avatar. But this, too, is a historical accident. In SimCity, you play a disembodied mayor who controls a growing city; you never see yourself. In chapter 11, I describe how our reliance on avatars constrains and changes how we interact with virtual worlds. The story of how online games came to be helps us understand not only what these games are but why they influence us as they do.

When arcade games appeared in bars and nightclubs in the 1970s, gaming was largely an adult pastime. In an analysis of three decades—1970 to 2000—of news articles on video games, Dmitri Williams, a professor of communication at the University of Southern California, has documented how media portrayal of gaming shifted dramatically in the 1980s. News and magazine articles began to associate gaming with male teenagers and to warn of the addictive and corrupting nature of video games: gaming was not only a gateway to deviance; gaming was deviant behavior.[1]

The reaction to gaming is not unique. Since the beginning of the twentieth century, the introduction of every communication medium has caused a moral panic centered on teens—movies in the 1920s, radio in the 1930s, comic books and rock and roll in the 1940s and 1950s, and so on. Following the publication of psychiatrist Fredric Wertham's *Seduction of the Innocent* in 1954, the media widely reported his unsubstantiated claim that reading comic books turned innocent boys into delinquents and criminals. After all, alarmist headlines sell papers. Cultural theorist Angela McRobbie has argued that moral panics encourage people to "turn away from the complexity and the visible social problems of everyday life . . . or to adopt a gung-ho 'something must be done about it' attitude." I would add that these panics are appealing because they reduce complex social problems into a simplistic model with one marginalized culprit. It's easier to put warning labels on video games than to address all the very real social, cultural, and psychological factors that lead to gun violence.[2]

Much as with comic books and rock and roll when they first appeared, the unrelenting media association between video games and teenagers led to the stereotype that only teenagers play video games. According to the news media, moreover, gaming wasn't just for teenagers: it was specifically for teenage boys. In addition, media reports repeatedly suggested that boys were biologically hardwired for violent video games. Williams quotes from a *Newsweek* article from 1989: "Nintendo speaks to something primal and powerful in their bloody-minded little psyches, the warrior instinct that in another culture would have sent them out on the hunt or the warpath." This alignment of gender, age, and deviance produces a simple yet powerful sound bite: video games turn boys into violent criminals. And it concisely reinforces multiple stereotypes: only teenage boys play video games, and they play these games because they enjoy violence. Online games actually combine two separate moral panics —worry about video games and fear of the Internet. And perhaps the emergence of online games is what allowed the moral panic of video games to continue into its third decade.

Even after thirty years, these stereotypes still strongly influence how we perceive gamers. In 2008, late-night talk show host Jimmy Kimmel played these stereotypes to great comedic effect when he cajoled actress Mila Kunis into divulging her *World of Warcraft* gaming habit: "I find it hard to believe . . . like, how fanatical are you about video games?" When Kunis asked Kimmel whether he had played *World of Warcraft*, his reply was, "I've not, but I've watched my son play it." Kimmel reinforced multiple stereotypes: only teenage boys, not women or grown men, should be playing video games.[3]

Before we can understand what people actually do in online games, we first need to acknowledge and debunk the pervasive stereotypes around who plays video games and why. Teenagers are actually the minority in online games. More important, online games are highly social, and gamers are not a monolithic category.

Debunking the Stereotypes

Despite common media portrayals, studies of thousands of online gamers—primarily English-speaking gamers in North America and western Europe—by different researchers across varied games and over the past decade have consistently found that players' average age is around thirty, with some players as young as eleven and some as old as sixty-eight. Only about 20 percent of these online gamers are teenage boys. Online games appeal to a broad age range. The majority of online gamers are adults in their twenties and thirties. Other findings show that many online gamers are leading normal adult lives outside of games. Fifty percent of online gamers work full-time, 36 percent are married, and 22 percent have children.[4]

Some player profiles gathered from my online study of more than fifty thousand players in the Daedalus Project illustrate the diversity of online gamers. Al is a sixty-year-old project manager working on a commercial airlines project in Houston. He started gaming in the 1980s with *Dungeons and Dragons*. Emre is twenty-seven, a graduate student in Germany. In *Star Wars Galaxies*, he plays a female Imperial pilot. In *World of Warcraft*, he's a "holier-than-thou Human Paladin." Jane is forty-six, a criminal defense lawyer from Ohio. She plays *EverQuest* with four people in her family. And Claire is a thirty-five-year-old computer technician and digital photo restoration artist from Idaho who has suffered from lupus for fifteen years and is unable to work. "Online games," she reports, "gave me a chance of socializing when I was unable to get out."

While there is a broad age range among online gamers, the gender stereotype is currently true. Only 20 percent of players in this game genre are women. We'll dive deeper into the possible causes of this significant gender difference in chapter 6, but this statistic makes clear that online games are currently more appealing to men. Despite this bias, the overall demographic composition of online games is diverse. In addition to high school students, there are college students, early adult professionals, and homemakers in their thirties, as well as war veterans and retirees. In some online games, a player group may span a sixty-year age difference. Teenagers who may feel a lack of control and agency in their everyday lives are suddenly able to work with adults as equals or even their superiors—something that almost never happens in the physical world. The stereotypical association of video games and teenagers is not only false but hinders our ability to understand how online games can be positive social spaces for younger players.[5]

Relatively few studies of online gamers outside the West have been conducted. These studies are also complicated by the fact that different online games tend to be popular in different regions—it's often not clear whether differences are due to culture or that particular game. *World of Warcraft*'s global appeal was unique in this sense and provided a way to compare demographics using the same game. Between 2010 and 2012, my colleagues and I gathered survey data from more than three thousand *World of Warcraft* gamers from mainland China, Hong Kong, Taiwan, the United States, and many countries in the European Union. We found that online gamers in the European Union closely tracked the demographics of gamers in the United States but that gamers from the Chinese countries had a very different profile. Their average age, twenty-two, was about ten years younger than online gamers in the West, with the majority of the Chinese players between the ages of twenty and twenty-four. There were also slightly fewer female players than in the West; 15 percent of the Chinese players were women. More research will be needed to understand what factors are responsible for these demographic differences, but these findings suggest that we need to be careful when extrapolating findings from Western gamers to gamers in other regions.[6]

Given the largely adult profile of online gamers in the West, studies on their typical play patterns reveal just how appealing these virtual environments can be. The average online gamer spends more than twenty hours a week playing online games. That's the equivalent of half a workweek spent in a virtual world. In one study, 9 percent of online gamers reported that they averaged forty hours or more each week. And 60 percent of players in that same study had at least on one occasion spent ten hours continuously in an online game. These statistics are also not skewed by the playing patterns of younger players. In two large studies of online gamers, one found no correlation between age and hours played each week; the other found that it was actually older players who spent more time in these virtual worlds. In short, older players in online games—in their thirties or older—do not spend any less time in these games than younger players. Although these statistics often appear alarming to nongamers, it's important to put them into perspective. According to a Nielsen report in 2012, the average American watches thirty-three hours of television each week. And most of us would probably admit that there was at least one time in our lives where we spent the entire day lounging in front of the TV.[7]

The rise of online games has accentuated the earlier stereotypes of antisocial deviance. After all, online games seem like the perfect escape; reclusive gamers can shut out the real world by logging into a digital fantasy world and cutting off all social connections. Again, studies of online gamers contradict these assumptions. One fourth of online gamers regularly play these games with a romantic partner or spouse; 19 percent of gamers do so with at least one family member (excluding spouses); and 70 percent of gamers do so with a friend they know in the physical world. Tallying across the categories, 80 percent of online gamers are regularly playing with someone they know outside the game. Instead of using virtual worlds to shut out the real world, gamers are using online games to socialize, keep in touch, and hang out with their friends and family. Here's how two gamers characterize their gaming experience:

> I've been getting together in a MMORPG with a very close friend of mine who moved recently. It gives us an opportunity to still "see" each other and be able to do things together, unlike just chatting (either on the phone or online) where we can't interact on the same level. Being able to "see" one another and then go hunting or hang around town feels much closer to getting together in real life than talking on the phone or e-mailing one another does. [*Realm Online*, male, 23]

> I regularly play online games with my husband. Knowing my husband's play style and him knowing mine, makes all the difference in our game enjoyment. We know what to expect from each other and rely on those things. Being able to play together keeps our relationship strong and playful, both in game and in real life. We always have something to talk about . . . the day to day RL grind and that ugly monster we had to deal with in game. =D [*A Tale in the Desert*, female, 44]

It is also worth noting that a family sitting together silently in front of the television is deemed socially acceptable, but if they chat and collaborate in a virtual world, this is stereotyped as being antisocial.[8]

In addition to their time investment, the emotional investment of players is important to consider. In one of the Daedalus Project surveys, 27 percent of online gamers indicated that the most rewarding or satisfying experience they had in the past week occurred in the game world. But there's a love-hate relationship here. In that same study, 33 percent of online gamers indicated that the most annoying or infuriating experience they had in the past week occurred in the game world. We see another indicator of this emotional investment in the relationships that emerge from these online games. Forty-one percent of online gamers felt that their in-game friendships—with people they first met in online games—were comparable to or better than those with their real-life friends. It may be tempting to frame these findings through a pathological escapist lens, but another interpretation is that these virtual worlds do a good job of creating engaging, social experiences that are highly memorable and forge relationships. In chapter 7, we'll hear from players who have fallen in love in online games.[9]

Why People Play

One of my favorite questions to ask online gamers is why they play these games. Understanding the diverse reasons why online gamers play these games is another way of moving beyond stereotypes. Players' answers vary tremendously. One player in *EverQuest* writes, "Overall, I enjoy taking on the role of a happy / silly little gnome who eats bugs," while another player in *Star Wars Galaxies* explains that he is "trying to establish a working corporation within the economic boundaries of the virtual world. Primarily, to learn more about how real world social theories play out in a virtual economy."

Richard Bartle's analysis of player types is a well-known taxonomy of why people enjoy online games. He categorizes players as achievers, socializers, killers (players who enjoy inflicting misery on others), and explorers (whether it's the geography or the game rules). My research in gameplay motivations built and expanded on Bartle's types. Statistical analysis of survey data from online gamers has consistently identified three clusters of gameplay motivations; these relate to achievement, social interaction, and immersion. The motivations within each cluster are highly correlated with one another and largely independent from motivations in the other two clusters. The achievement cluster focuses on different ways of gaining power within the context of the game. The social interaction cluster is about different ways of relating to other people in the game. And the immersion cluster is about different ways of becoming a part of the story.[10]

These aren't separate categories that players fall into but rather the building blocks that allow us to understand individual players. Thus, most players have high scores on one or two clusters while having average or low scores on the remaining clusters. The holistic configuration of these three building blocks traces out the unique profile of each gamer. These motivation clusters also do not imply that achievement activities are always nonsocial (as an example). After all, a player may have high scores on both the achievement and social motivations at the same time (that is, a player interested in guilds and end-game raiding), but the building blocks indicate that this is only one of many possible configurations. Only by specifying the underlying individual building blocks can the full matrix of possibilities be mapped out.

In terms of the achievement motivations, power can be satisfying in different ways. For some players, the satisfaction comes from a sense of progress in the construct of the game—leveling up and gradually becoming more powerful.

> I feel achievement is my greatest motivation for playing. I can't wait to level again and get that new ability or skill or awesome weapon, but I never want to hit max level. [World of Warcraft, male, 28]

> It gives me the illusion of progress, I know that. I hate the level of frustrated progress in the real world so I play the game and lvl up instead. [World of Warcraft, male, 34]

In contrast, other players do not care about the sense of progress. What they care about is being as powerful as possible. For them, it's not about the journey but about the destination. Social recognition is also often important for these players.

> I basically play these games to become the most powerful force the game can allow. I want the best of the best items and people to truly respect my play style. I want to become a legend among players within the virtual mmorpg world! [Dark Age of Camelot, male, 25]

For others, it is power over other players that is truly satisfying. This might be driven by the desire to be on top or the desire to overpower and dominate weaker players. These players often seek out competitive, player-versus-player activities.

> Being the best is most fun. I have always been extremely competitive, I grew up with a brother who is very competitive, so I have been used to competition since birth. . . . I have learned to find satisfaction in winning and love all games, board, sports and electronic games, because in all games u have winners and losers. [World of Warcraft, male, 18]

And finally, for some players, the joy in playing online games comes from dissecting and understanding all the numbers and rules in the game. This then allows them to plan out and optimize their character.

> Just recently, I spent three days working out a jewelry / armor template that would allow me to max as many things as possible for my last set of armor when I hit max level. [Dark Age of Camelot, female, 23]

> I had created 30+ templates and spent literally 40+ spare hours creating templates at catacombs and other sites to make sure I had the best build. Then when I finally got there and it all fit into place—that made it all worth it. [World of Warcraft, male, 25, describing his earlier experience in Dark Age of Camelot]

For players who enjoy social interaction, online games might be viewed as a large chat room in which there is always someone to chat with, always new people to meet.

> I love to talk to people, all of the time. I generally am talking to several people at a time, and feel slightly uncomfortable in silent groups. My friends list grows often. When I played the original EverQuest, I maxed my friends list (100 players) at one point and had to delete a few alts of friends. [EverQuest II, male, 17]

On the other hand, some players who enjoy this social ambience aren't necessarily interested in developing deep or meaningful relationships.

> I like interacting with other people, chatting, etc., but . . . I have a pretty low desire to make what I consider "good friends" as that would involve a real-life component I'd rather keep separate from my game playing. [EverQuest II, male, 39]

Now contrast this with other players who are open to or specifically interested in becoming good friends with people they meet online.

> It's fun having friends all over the world, you can learn from the way they live and do things. That's what I mostly enjoy about meeting

others in game. To befriend people and get to know them, hopefully building a lasting friendship even when one of us does end up giving up on whatever game we're playing. [*EverQuest II*, female, 19]

I'm currently sitting in Las Vegas typing this using the network of a friend I met via EverQuest. . . . We met IRL [in real life] last summer when she had reason to visit Boston (I live in Connecticut), and now I'm visiting her for several days. My dearest female friend I also met via EverQuest. . . . I not only spend every Xmas with her and her husband (4 times so far) but also visit her for a week every couple of months. They don't even EQ any more but the friendship continues strong and growing. [*EverQuest*, female, 61]

The last motivation that falls into the social interaction cluster is teamwork. For these players, what is fun is working with other players and being part of a team.

A strong motivation for me is working with other people and existing within a perfect and efficient group. The aims of this group are not important, we could be grinding or camping a spawn to get an item for someone, when everything goes perfect, no communication is needed, and everyone just does what they should exactly as it should be done, I just feel great. . . . Interacting with people and being able to depend on them, and be depended on by them . . . that's why I play. [*World of Warcraft*, male, 20]

For players interested in immersion, there are a variety of ways to become connected with the story of the online game. Some players create in-depth background stories for their characters that tether them in some way to other players or the story arcs in the game.

It's important for me to have backstories for my characters before I really enjoy playing them. For example, I know that Trigger, my dwarven rogue, is the younger sister of my husband's character's (Hawthorne) best friend. Thus when Trigger plays, it's with a great deal of enthusiasm and not necessarily a great deal of sense. When Trig

and Hawthorne group together, there's a great deal of friendly bickering and /bonk going on. I think it's a replacement for the acting I did
in school, which is so hard to fit into my life as an adult. [*World of Warcraft*, female, 36]

I've been playing as a Night Elf Druid who's older than dirt, but has
been hibernating for millennia. It's been fun to play out her first encounters with humans, gnomes, and orcs, none of whom existed
when she went to sleep. I've been playing her as the type that's incredibly wise, formerly very powerful, but somewhat confused about the
modern world. [*World of Warcraft*, male, 23]

These character stories often lead to improvised, in-character interactions with other characters, referred to as role-playing. Although
nongamers might assume that all online gamers role-play, given that
the game genre is described as role-playing games, this form of improvised storytelling is actually a niche activity. The label "role-
playing" was devised to mark the shift from army squadrons to individual characters in miniature wargaming, not the importance of
storytelling. "Role-playing" thus has two very different meanings in
online games. In *World of Warcraft*, the niche status of role-playing is
made clear by the fact that only a handful of the hundreds of available
servers are explicitly labeled as role-playing servers.

Other players interested in stories may instead be fascinated by the
stories of the game world—its characters, histories, leaders, and
cities. These players are interested in exploring the world and learning as much as they can about the lore of the game.

I love the stories around the new Everquest. I went from zone to zone
talking to people trying to figure out how we arrived where we are in
the story—500 years later and the moon of Luclin now gone. Where
are those frogloks? I am anxious about getting through certain zones
because I want to see/do more. [*EverQuest*, female, 37]

> I do enjoy exploring, but what I enjoy even more is the creation and participation in a story. Exploring the world is a large part of that. I'm a big reader . . . fantasy, sci-fi, and interesting biography. When I'm having my "best times" in game is when I'm pursuing a quest or participating in some grand adventure. [*EverQuest II*, male, 30]

Of course, for some players, the sense of being transported into a living, breathing fantasy world is in and of itself already incredibly appealing.

> I don't necessarily Role-Play a lot, but feeling like I'm "in" the game is really fun. For example, in EverQuest, I felt like I was just playing a random computer game. Whereas with World of Warcraft I really feel like I'm involved because there's a rich history and I know a lot of the history about it. [*World of Warcraft*, male, 18]

Online games appeal to a broad demographic because they tap into a wide set of gameplay motivations. Even in a dungeon group of five players, there might be a player who just wants to slay the dragon, another player who wants to know how the story ends, two brothers in different countries playing together to spend time with each other, and a player who is injecting some much-needed humor through role-playing antics. These virtual worlds allow players to engage in very different kinds of gameplay side by side.

The Paradox of Escape

Online games are like school in many ways. Both provide predefined rewards for a set of highly constrained and objectively measured activities. If you write all your letters between the rows of gray lines, you get a silver star. If you get ten silver stars, you can trade up for a gold star. If you want to get into a good college, you need to get a certain score on the SAT. Wherever you are in the education treadmill, you know exactly where you are, where you'll be next, and how to get there. For about sixteen years of our lives, this is the model of progress we are all taught. And then we're let loose into the real world, where these rules go away. Goals are no longer defined for you. Performance in many jobs has no clear objective measure. Sometimes your boss takes the credit, someone else gets promoted instead, or you reach a dead-end within the company. The real world is tough, and it's often unfair.

Not so in online games. Everyone who kills the evil bandit gets the same amount of experience points. Goals are clear, predefined, and fair. Your achievements are displayed in a multitude of easy-to-read progress bars.

> In an MMORPG you can see a consistent progression of development in your skills. You are getting better at a steady rate. In RL you don't level up when you get ahead, it isn't as obvious. [*World of Warcraft*, male, 31]

> While I personally own and run a successful small business, and have enjoyed reaching milestones and goals I've set for myself, they come fewer and farther between than I NEED, and so, playing online games allows me to find a positive outlet for that need to achieve on a regular basis. [*World of Warcraft*, female, 37]

We don't play games just because they fit our gameplay motivations, we also play them for deeply human and cultural reasons. For many players, like the successful small business owner, this can be therapeutic. Online games can provide a cheap, convenient way of feeling progress. On the other hand, playing online games primarily to escape from real-life problems can easily lead to a vicious cycle.

> I have been out of work now for over a month and now find myself in a stressful, depressed state that is only quelled when I am playing Ever-Quest, because it's easy to forget about real world troubles and

problems, but the problem is when you get back to the real world, problems and troubles have become bigger, and it's a bad, bad cycle. [EverQuest, male, 26]

I was having financial troubles and marital problems as well. I could ignore my real life and escape into EverQuest. This wasn't for the fun, it was a "need" that I felt to not deal with my life responsibly and EverQuest was my chosen method of "drugging" myself into blissful ignorance. [EverQuest, male, 33]

Studies have consistently shown that the gamers who are most at risk for problematic gaming—gaming that makes it difficult for someone to manage their life—are those who are suffering from depression and social anxiety. In this light, problematic gaming arises from failed attempts at self-treatment. Players who play to escape are precisely the ones who become increasingly saddled with reality. Crucially, once these psychological well-being variables are taken into account, the effect that game variables (such as gameplay motivations) have on problematic gaming is marginal. In fact, gaming can be beneficial when it's part of a healthy palette of social interactions. Family members who play online games together report more family communication time and better communication quality. Dmitri Williams often uses a phrase that succinctly captures these differences in outcomes: "The rich get richer and the poor get poorer." These findings underscore two related and important points: gaming can augment existing social networks, and well-adjusted gamers are largely not at risk of problematic gaming.[11]

As big as the stereotypical jock-versus-nerd divide is in high school, there are many similarities between football and online games. Both are social activities that take place in a cordoned-off portion of reality. In these virtual worlds, different rules and objectives come into play. Players take on fantasy roles that have functional meaning only in the fantasy world. They are awarded points for arbitrarily defined tasks. Teamwork and competition play a large role in both games.

On the other hand, there is a tremendous difference in how people interpret tragedies that occur in these two games. Between 1994 and 2009, an average of three football players died each year in the United States from overheating, usually during intensive training in summer. When such a death occurs, the media often approach the subject with a holistic perspective: they question whether the coach set an unreasonably exhausting regimen, whether the parents saw warning signs, and whether the school reviewed the coach's history thoroughly; they wonder why the school mandates practice in the hot summer months and how the team physicians took into account the idiosyncratic health profiles of different players. And in no time during all this introspection does anyone suggest football is addictive and that a new pathological designation should be created for football. A leather ball is too low-tech and too mainstream to be useful for instilling paranoia.[12]

We cherry-pick addictions. Some people accumulate cats in their houses until their lives are overrun with toxic animal waste, but there are no dramatic news stories warning us that cats are addictive. Certainly, some gamers spend too much time playing online games and this leads to problems with their work, relationships, or health, but the label "online gaming addiction" is a rhetorical sleight of hand that distracts us from the actual psychological problems from which these gamers suffer. When we focus our attention on the technology, we take the person out of the equation. These labels are a disingenuous rebranding of common coping mechanisms stemming from depression and social anxiety; they sideline the fact that taking the technology away won't resolve these underlying psychological problems.

Whether it's the frivolous nature of video games, the people who play online games, or online gaming addiction, our cultural stereotypes often distract us from the reality of gaming. And by focusing our attention on these myths of bad inputs and outputs—delinquent male teenagers, antisocial behavior, and gaming addiction—these self-serving cultural stories have encouraged us to ignore what actually happens inside these online games. In the next part of the book, I'll draw from different aspects of online games to explain why the promise of escape and freedom in virtual worlds is illusory. Our psychological baggage and social stereotypes follow us into these fantasy worlds.

In EverQuest there were several folks in my guild who believed if their characters got drunk enough they would actually be teleported to a special location. I think this rumor started because somebody got so drunk they couldn't tell where they were walking (since being drunk warps the way the game draws the graphics) and got stuck in a weird place under Freeport or Qeynos. So these guys kept getting smashed on long camps to try and go to this "special" location, which really screwed us one time when the mob we wanted appeared but half of the group was too wasted to attack it. No matter how much others tried to convince them that there was no special place, they never stopped believing it was true.

[*World of Warcraft*, male, 36]

In the early parts of online games, and even after many hours of playing, players are often only tapping a few keys on their keyboard repeatedly. The game provides incentives for these repetitive gestures whether this is leveling up or finding a rare weapon on a slain monster. From the perspective of an outsider, who hasn't been carefully trained by the game to desire these virtual incentives, many online games may appear tedious and boring. In fact, gamers themselves have a word for the repetitive monster killing that slowly levels them up: they call it *grinding*.

A well-studied psychological principle called *operant conditioning* helps us understand how a system of rewards can make an inherently uninteresting task appealing. In its simplest form, the principle seems obvious. If you reward a person for performing a certain behavior, he or she is more likely to repeat that behavior. The way you provide rewards matters a great deal. Imagine training your dog. After a dog has successfully learned the "sit" command, you might use a fixed schedule and provide a treat every two times the dog follows the command. Or you might provide a treat after a random number of successful "sits." Studies have shown that the latter schedule is best for maintaining behavior. If a fixed schedule is ever broken, even accidentally, it is easily detected, and the behavior quickly ceases. A broken variable schedule isn't immediately obvious, and the behavior continues.[1]

Another important lesson is that small, rapid rewards can be used to shape incremental progression toward a complex behavior. Your dog will never spontaneously perform complicated tricks such as jumping through a hoop and then running up some stairs to fetch a colored balloon. How, then, to provide a reward to a behavior that doesn't spontaneously manifest itself? To train the dog to perform this trick, the trainer first rewards the dog for moving toward the hoop, then another reward for jumping through the hoop, then another reward for moving toward the stairs, and so forth. Once the dog has learned all the steps, then the dog's owner can maintain the complex trick with just one reward for each complete run.

Online games employ many operant conditioning principles, through both historical trial and error as well as deliberate design. In the early part of the game, many small rewards help players understand the basic paths of advancement. A lowly level 1 character can kill a rat in ten seconds, and after killing ten rats, the character has already become a level 2 character. This initial shaping helps new players learn about combat, monsters, leveling, and equipment. Gradually, the game offers rewards less frequently. Monsters take longer to kill, and it takes twenty-five monster kills to reach level 3, and then a hundred kills to reach level 4. Very soon, it takes hours of repetitive play to reach the next level, and only rarely is a useful piece of equipment found on a monster.

To facilitate the study of operant conditioning in pigeons and lab rats, B. F. Skinner, the father of radical behaviorism, developed a self-contained testing apparatus, an operant conditioning chamber, better known as a Skinner box. These boxes of wood and glass give the researcher a clear view of the interior. Inside the box are levers that a pigeon or a lab rat can press on, as well as a food-dispensing mechanism. The researcher can release a food pellet on a predetermined schedule after the animal presses a lever.

Although online games clearly rely on much more than operant conditioning, the overlapping elements are undeniable. Online games shape a new player's behavior toward complex button presses using a schedule of rewards that is tightly coupled to specific actions. The game rewards correct behaviors rapidly until the behavior is learned, at which point the behavior can be sustained with less frequent rewards. Many rare items, whether magical equipment or quest items, are dropped by monsters using a variable schedule. You may know that killing the glowing monkey will make it drop a glowing shard, but you don't know how many glowing monkeys you will have to kill before that shard appears.

Skinner is well known for his theory of operant conditioning, but in a quirkier study, he induced superstition in pigeons. His goal was to show that complex human phenomena could be entirely explained by observable and measurable behaviors without recourse to internal cognitive variables such as desires, thoughts, or feelings. As you can imagine, Skinner was no fan of Freud, whose psyche (that is, id, ego, and superego) and defense mechanisms Skinner regarded as impossible to observe and requiring further explanation.

In Skinner's study, he placed pigeons into Skinner boxes and gave them food pellets using a reward schedule. The pigeons received a food pellet every fifteen seconds, no matter what they did. When the food was released, the pigeon was rewarded for whatever random behavior it was performing. As the bird repeated this behavior because of the reward, the food dropped again, and the behavior was further reinforced. In six of the eight pigeons tested, a clear superstitious behavior resulted. In Skinner's words,

> One bird was conditioned to turn counter-clockwise about the cage, making two or three turns between reinforcements. Another repeatedly thrust its head into one of the upper corners of the cage. A third developed a "tossing" response, as if placing its head beneath an invisible bar and lifting it repeatedly. Two birds developed a pendulum motion of the head and body. . . . Another bird was conditioned to make incomplete pecking or brushing movements directed toward but not touching the floor.

These pigeons behaved as if their ritualized actions caused the food to appear, even though this was not the case. The birds repeated the behaviors five to six times every fifteen seconds. Thus, even though only about 20 percent of the superstitious behavior directly led to food, the intermittent appearance of food was sufficient to sustain the behavior. One of the birds performed ten thousand ritual movements without any food reward before the behavior subsided.[2]

High school students do not perform much better than pigeons; a fixed-interval reward led high schoolers to perform elaborate compositions on a piano keyboard. Similar superstitions appear quite often in online games. This makes sense because online games are a kind of Skinner box, and often the cause of rare but highly desirable game outcomes is not immediately obvious. When a superstitious behavior emerges, it is often inadvertently reinforced by the game. The abundance of levers and food pellet flavors in an online game makes it easy to confuse the underlying causal relations between actions and rewards.[3]

Spawn Dances

When a player kills a monster, it reappears after some time so that it can be killed again. Otherwise, monsters would quickly become extinct. This reappearance is known as *spawning* or *respawning*. Some monsters have fixed and rapid spawn rates (for example, ten seconds after death), while other have random and highly variable spawn rates (anywhere between one and a thousand minutes after death). In the original *EverQuest*, some monsters had spawn times of an hour or even up to six hours or more. Some rare monsters had *placeholder* spawns that further complicated things. A placeholder is a common monster that holds the place of the rare mob and thus prevents the rare mob from spawning until the placeholder is killed. To make things worse, many monsters did not have fixed spawn locations but could spawn in one of several locations on the map. This made it incredibly difficult for one player to know whether the rare monster he or she was waiting for had spawned or whether another player had killed it already. This slow, chaotic pacing was not a unique feature of rare monsters; it was a fact of life in *EverQuest*. A standard monster that took thirty seconds to kill had a respawn time of several minutes— time during which players often had nothing to do. In these many moments of mixed tedium and anticipation, spawn rituals were born. One prevalent superstition was the existence of an "antispawn" radius.

> In EverQuest, many players were under the impression that the respawn mechanic for monsters / NPCs [non-player characters] took into account players' positions. So when people were fighting things in

dungeons, they'd often leave whatever room they were in for a bit because they felt that the room wouldn't respawn while they were there. [EverQuest, male, 24]

It was widely believed that the game designers had implemented an "anti-camp radius" around major spawns, such that the mobs would not spawn if people were within the radius. Of course, no one knew exactly what the extent of this radius was, so more risk-averse people would camp further and further from the spawn point in order to avoid the radius. The developers at Verant found this so funny (there was no anti-camp radius) that they added a comment during some loading screens, "Checking anti-camp radius," just to mess with these players. [EVE Online, male, 31]

Another superstition was that the corpses of monsters were placeholders and needed to be looted quickly to speed up respawns.

In Everquest it was a belief that you needed to loot all the corpses of everything in order for more mobs to spawn. This of course is untrue. The mobs spawn on a fairly precise timer and have nothing to do with crowding around the spawn area. [City of Heroes, female, 37]

Finally, many players developed ritual "dances" for spawning:

My favorite rituals would probably be the various "spawn dances" in EverQuest. . . . They varied wildly—some people had special gear sets they used, others had sets and sequences of movements and animations (via animated emotes, spellcasting, terrain), ways to move or not move (must stay sitting, still, as much as possible; or must move continually / every X seconds), etc. [World of Warcraft, male, 23]

Some players would sit and stand rapidly while strafing back and forth. Others would crouch and run in circles or figure-eight patterns. Jumping seemed also to be a common theme. Seeing a full group of six characters dancing in this manner shortly before a mob was to spawn was very funny. I think that it sometimes was done as a joke, but I knew some players who swore by its success. [EverQuest, male, 28]

In the same way that pigeons dance for food in boxes, people dance for monsters in online games.

Dungeon Seeding

In World of Warcraft, there is a chance that bosses will drop highly valuable pieces of equipment in difficult dungeons. Dungeons in World of Warcraft are known as instances because player teams each enter their own version of the dungeon. So if fifty different teams are running the Molten Core dungeon, the game creates fifty parallel, independent versions of the dungeon, one for each team. Bosses in the game have set loot tables—that is, different probabilities for a predetermined set of loot, of which several may drop if the boss is killed. Because different classes use different types of equipment (for example, rogues can use daggers, druids can use staves) in the game, many players often leave a dungeon run empty-handed. Boss drops are thus low-probability events with highly desirable outcomes that elicit superstitious behavior.

> There is a widely held belief that instances are "seeded" despite lack of evidence and even a direct denial from Blizzard. Seeded refers to the person who starts the group or raid, and it is believed that the class of that person directly impacts what class specific loot will drop. I.E. if a warrior starts the Molten Core raid invites, more druid and warlock gear will drop. If a priest starts the invites, more warrior and mage loot will drop, etc. [World of Warcraft, male, 33]

> Blizzard consistently states that loot drops are completely random. Yet a lot of people don't believe this because some items drop over and over when under one Master Looter and different items would drop over and over when under a different Master Looter. [World of Warcraft, male, 34]

A variant of this belief is that certain characters are luckier or have better loot tables if they are allowed to seed the instance.

> We have a particular guildmate who insists that when he enters the dungeon instance first, better loot will tend to drop. Granted, when he has entered first, we've received some very nice, even legendary items in World of Warcraft, but to think he's somehow affecting the loot table by being the first to enter is a bit much. [World of Warcraft, male, 30]

> [There is] the belief that certain classes seed certain loot in PvE instances within World of Warcraft and that certain players are "lucky" seeders in terms of an increased high-level loot drop rate. Sometimes, raids have been held up until these lucky seeders or a member of a certain class arrives at the instance entrance. [World of Warcraft, female, 33]

> Silliest is that a particular person provides some sort of luck to getting loot—that one person is responsible for the "seed" being good or bad. [World of Warcraft, female, 49]

In short, some characters in online games come to be viewed as being inherently lucky.

Lucky Charms

In addition to the belief that certain people are lucky, there are pervasive superstitions around items that confer luck. The specific items differ from game to game, but these superstitions take the same general form.

> In World of Warcraft there are 2 items that are said to bring luck to the owner. These are the "Rabbit's foot" and the "Lucky charm." These items drop off common mobs around the world. There is a group of players that strongly believes that carrying around one or more of these items increases your luck in loot drops. People often use specific events

and strokes of luck to prove that they "work." I myself don't believe it has any effect at all but still have a "Rabbit's foot" in my inventory because you never know. [*World of Warcraft*, male, 41]

[Some believe] that carrying or owning items whose names implied good luck (Fortune Egg, Millionaire's desk, 4 Leaf Mandragora Bud) would increase drop rates despite no evidence to prove this. I'll admit to doing it myself! [*Final Fantasy XI*, female, 25]

In Anarchy Online, some people believed that wearing certain gear was the way to gain certain drops and would spend hours farming gear so that they could farm other gear. [*Anarchy Online*, male, 33]

What's particularly intriguing in this set of narratives is that some players explicitly state that they do not believe in the superstition but follow it anyway.

Over-Enchanting

Another type of high-risk action occurs in games in which players are allowed to *over-enchant* equipment. In many games, players can enchant an item to give it a bonus, whether to combat skills or the character's traits. In some of these games, the player can enchant the same item multiple times. Once the player has reached a certain threshold, there is a chance that the item may be destroyed in the process. Over-enchanting refers to the process of enchanting an item beyond its safety threshold. The risk of item destruction is proportionate to the number of existing enchantments over the threshold. Given the daunting risk of destroying a valuable piece of equipment, over-enchanting is a high-risk gamble ripe for superstitions.

In Lineage II . . . enchanting to +3 is risk-free. However, at +4 and above the item has a chance of breaking, causing you to lose a lot of money. Many people have gone so far as to quit the game or reroll after blowing up their ultra-expensive gear. A very prevalent superstition is for people to take the item into a church when attempting to over-enchant it. Many people, if they were successful over-enchanting an item at a certain spot, will return to that spot every time they need to over-enchant. [*Lineage 2*, female, 24]

In addition to location-based superstitions, ritual behaviors conducted before over-enchanting have also developed in other games.

In Ultima Online it has been stated many times by the Dev[eloper]s that "eating" does nothing to enhance the characters' abilities. Many players still choose to eat before they try to do some specific crafting where the risk of destroying an item for example is high. [*Ultima Online*, female, 45]

Some go to only a particular NPC—some will not only upgrade at only a certain NPC, but also upgrade ONLY within a certain time period— some do it ONLY while standing on a "lucky" spot, yet others believe that the secret is to wait there patiently till someone comes in . . . then wait for him to fail . . . they believe that their attempt will be 100 percent successful if it follows on the heels of someone succeeding. I personally am guilty of a fairly weird ritual myself—I tend to strip off all equipment I am carrying and log off in between EVERY attempt to refine my gear. :) [*Ragnarok Online*, male, 29]

Here's a final example of a crafting superstition from *Final Fantasy XI* that also hints at why it is so difficult for superstitions to go away once they begin.

One of the most persistent superstitions (and for all I know, it might be true) was that facing in certain cardinal directions would affect how your crafting came out. It was the perfect superstition, because it took so little effort to follow that even if it wasn't true, you didn't lose anything by acting as if it was true. [*Final Fantasy XI*, female, 23]

Treasure Negotiation

Superstitions, pervasive across online games, develop wherever a high-risk or low-probability event leads to a highly desirable outcome. This scenario is common in online games, whether it is valuable loot from a boss, over-enchanting a weapon, or having a rare monster spawn. Many of these superstitions persist despite limited or anecdotal evidence or even direct refutation by game designers.

In *Dungeons and Dragons Online*, diplomacy is one of many skills that a character can learn. Game designers intended for players to use the skill on computer-controlled characters, allowing for alternative conversation paths as well as the distraction of enemies during combat. A programming error made it possible for players to use the diplomacy skill on treasure chests, although doing so had no impact on the game. Heather Sinclair, a member of the development team, has publicly discussed the aftermath of this programming error.

> From beta all the way through months into launch players were CON-VINCED that if you used the diplomacy skill on a chest it would improve the loot you got. . . . This was SO widespread that you literally could not get in a pickup group without them querying about the diplomacy skills of the party and someone forcing everyone to wait while the highest diplomacy skill player cringed before the chest sufficiently.

This superstition became so pervasive that the game developers decided to debunk it publicly. The public statements, however, had the opposite effect:

> No matter how many times we posted on the forums that this was a myth and it doesn't do anything, they kept doing it. It got so bad our community relations manager even put it in his [forum signature]. Finally we made chests an invalid target for the diplomacy skill, then

players whined that all the points they put into diplomacy were worthless because we "nerfed" the skill!

Not only are superstitions prevalent in online games, but some are also incredibly resilient to debunking.[4]

The Social Reinforcement of Superstitions

In several of the player narratives, people who claim they don't believe in the superstition nevertheless carry out the superstitious behavior, just in case. Social factors also help sustain these superstitions. The most significant is the relative low cost of the ritual compared to the relative high value of the potential reward, especially in situations in which the team members have nothing else to do to fill the time. After all, if you get to run a difficult dungeon only once a week, what's the harm in trying something that takes just thirty seconds?

> Generally the experimentation is harmless enough that it is at least permitted by skeptics of the theory. [*World of Warcraft*, male, 24]

There is also the relative cost of trying to debunk a superstition. In a typed chat setting, it takes much more time and effort to argue and attempt to debunk a superstition than to simply follow along, even if you don't believe in the behavior.

If the potential outcome is negative rather than positive, risk aversion comes into play. For example, there are superstitions that make a boss easier to kill and thus decrease the odds of a *raid wipe*—the obliteration of the entire team by a tough encounter.

> "Hey kids, don't use curse of weakness on Gandling, because he starts teleporting people a ton faster . . . ." But nobody wanted to try it out; I remember actually offering to pay people a gold each to let me try . . . and they refused; . . . people are very pious when it comes to respecting these technological taboos. [*World of Warcraft*, male, 23]

In Skinner's pigeon study, superstitious behaviors persisted even though they did not produce food 80 percent of the time. Even a low contingency rate was sufficient to sustain a superstition. The same is true in online games. After all, a ritual that produces highly beneficial outcomes 20 percent of the time is still worth performing. Indeed, probabilistic superstitions are hard to debunk without a large experimental data set, which few players would have the time or tenacity to collect.

> If it worked some of the time, it was enough for the group in question to continue to think that the process they were following was crucial to the success of whatever it was they were doing. [*EverQuest II*, male, 36]

With a group of five people, the likelihood that the superstition has recently been true (that is, reinforced) for any one team member is very high. This secondhand reinforcement also creates the illusion of a much higher success rate.

Old Dogs and New Tricks

Superstition in online games reveals something very important and fundamental about how people interact with new technology. To help us unravel this, let me describe a study that changed how we think about human-computer interaction.

Are people polite to computers? Given that computers are inanimate objects without feelings, this question may seem ridiculous. But a study conducted at Stanford University in 1996 showed that people interact with computers as if they had feelings. Communication scholars Clifford Nass and Byron Reeves had college students take a tutoring session from a standard desktop computer. The session was about different facts of American culture, such as the percentage of American teenagers who kiss on the first date, and included a quiz on a set of questions the computer had not tutored students on, followed by a scoring session in which the computer went through the students' responses and let them know how they performed. The students were then asked to complete an evaluation of the tutoring session either on the same computer or on a different computer.

When a family member asks you what you think of his or her cooking at a family gathering, you tend to be polite and avoid offending that person. If someone else pulled you aside and asked you the same question, you'd probably be more honest. It turns out that people obey this politeness rule even when interacting with computers. The researchers found that students gave more favorable evaluations if they filled the form out on the same computer that tutored them. Students who filled out evaluations on a different computer gave less positive responses. Given that these college students were all familiar with computers, they did not consciously believe that computers had feelings. Instead, as Reeves and Nass argue, users rely on existing social norms when interacting with new technology. And we do this because our brains lack the cognitive resources to create and follow entirely new social protocols for every novel class of technology we encounter. When a computer asks us to evaluate its cooking (so to speak), we subconsciously treat it as if it were a person asking us, and the politeness rule is triggered. Without even being aware of it, we treat computers as if they had feelings and could be hurt emotionally by our remarks.[5]

As another example of how we fall back on existing social norms even in new technological spaces, consider the notion of personal space in virtual worlds. In the physical world, the amount of personal space we give another person depends a lot on whom we're talking to and what we're talking about. Intimacy, for example, can be expressed either with eye contact or by moving closer to another person. When one of these cues is accidentally triggered, such as when we are crammed next to strangers in an elevator, we modulate the other cue to maintain the appropriate level of intimacy. Thus, in an elevator, we turn away from and avoid eye contact with the people next to us to defuse the cues of uncomfortable intimacy. In a study my colleagues and I conducted in *Second Life*, a virtual world in which users can create their own content, we wondered whether people moving around with the mouse and keyboard in digital avatars would nevertheless conform to these physical norms. And it turned out that this modulation of eye contact and personal space indeed occurs in *Second Life*; people standing close to each other in *Second Life* are less likely to be looking directly at the other person. Instead of developing new social norms, we fall back on the ones we've learned from the physical world.[6]

The same is true for superstitions. False contingencies trigger superstitious behaviors around highly desirable rewards, whether we're talking about pigeons in Skinner boxes or people in online games. For pigeons, this is food pellets. For online gamers, the rewards are magical items, rare monster spawns, or over-enchanting equipment. When a superstitious idea emerges, it can be inadvertently reinforced, and then social dynamics such as low relative cost help it spread across a community. And once a superstitious ritual spreads, it takes on a life of its own, and not even the direct refutation by game developers can quash the superstition.

Our digital bodies are fluid, mutable with the click of the mouse. Our fantasy worlds, with their elven druids and galactic starships, seem far removed from the physical world and infinitely malleable. But the reality is quite strange and sobering. Even if virtual worlds were tabula rasa, we are encumbered with a great deal of cognitive baggage. Our brains are hardwired with many mental shortcuts to help us make sense of the world. We simply do not have the time to carefully process every piece of information that comes our way. To cope with this inundation of information, our brains have developed automated heuristics that filter and preprocess this information for us. Thus, when we encounter new media and technological devices, we fall back on the existing rules and norms we know. We react to computers as if they were human and had feelings. And when we enter virtual worlds, this mental baggage hitches a ride with us. We react to digital bodies the way we react to physical bodies. And the same psychological triggers that lead to superstitions in Skinner's pigeons lead us to develop superstitions in online games. This is an example of the Proteus Paradox: how our brains work doesn't change when we slip into a digital body. In a fully digital technological construct meticulously built from rational, precise program code, the irony is that superstitions persist and flourish.[7]

The Supernatural in Online Games

The likelihood is high that most of these habits are just superstitions. On the other hand, although it is easy and standard for game developers to use random number generators throughout a game, it takes only two lines of program code to make a four-leaf clover bring you good luck on Tuesdays. And although we are unlikely to settle any debates about the existence of God in the physical world, there actually is an omnipotent, omniscient god in online games known as the game developer, who can and does change the rules and bend the laws of nature. Causal relations in online games can be magical, defying physical laws. There is no logical or scientific reason why a four-leaf clover would bring you good luck in the physical world, but there is a rational and scientifically sound reason for why this might happen in an online game.

In fact, the reason why players in Final Fantasy XI believe that cardinal directions and moon phases have an impact on crafting is because moon phases actually do have an impact on certain well-documented aspects of the game. For example, some magical equipment is enhanced when the moon is in its crescent phase (both waxing and waning).[8]

> Final Fantasy XI's crafting system was particularly ripe for superstitions, because the parts of the system that were verified were wacky enough that anything might have been true. [Final Fantasy XI, female, 23]

Hidden rules not only perplex gamers, they also perplex game developers. The interwoven complexities of program code make it difficult even for game developers to identify non-obvious bugs. This was the case in Asheron's Call. When a few players began to complain that their characters were perpetually unlucky and unfairly targeted by monsters, it was easy for the game developer, Turbine, to brush them off and claim that it could find no such bug. On the face of it, the notion of monster-haunted characters did seem like digital hypochondria. In the game community, this rumor was referred to as the Wi Flag, named after a character named Wi who widely discussed his torment. And everyone had a good laugh out of it for a few months, until it was revealed by Turbine that there was indeed a bug.

Our developers at Turbine initially answered these complaints by saying that they could find no such bug. . . . Easy culprits, such as a mal-
functioning random-number generator, were eventually dismissed. But
our search went on. . . . And then one day, long after most people had
learned to either forget or ignore the Wi Flag, the answer was found. . . .
We hope it is of some interest to those of you who have long been
afflicted with this terrible burden.[9]

In *Asheron's Call*, monsters choose whom to attack at any given moment based on metrics such as who attacked it last or who is doing
the most damage, but these metrics do not apply when a group of
players first appears within a monster's attack radius. Turbine's code
for the game had an error in this part of the decision-making algorithm. Monsters were more likely to attack players at the beginning of the group list. A character's identification number, perma-
nent and assigned during character creation, determined the sorting
order in the group list by mistake and, thus, the likelihood of attack.
In other words, some players in *Asheron's Call* were indeed perpetually
unlucky and haunted by monsters.

Whether directly implemented by game developers or inadvertently introduced into the game via bugs, magical causality is not
only plausible in online games, but we can actually point to specific
instances of it. Moon phases can affect your performance. People can
be born unlucky. And even though magical causality in online games
is uncommon, believing in the supernatural in online games is not
entirely irrational. Thus, online games not only hijack our psychological wiring to encourage superstitious beliefs and rituals, but the
plausibility of supernatural beliefs helps propel and sustain these
superstitions. Our social training and brain wiring follow us into
these new worlds. We think of technology as something that pro-
motes rationality, but technological constructs can actually promote

superstition. And as we're playing games, we're also being played, driven to dance in virtual boxes.

Superstitions in online games reveal several surprising aspects of game design. First, game designers often don't have complete control over the social systems they create. In the case of *Dungeons and Dragons Online*, players rejected the developers' statements that conflicted with their own beliefs on negotiating with treasure chests. And second, players are actually creating a great deal of game content even in the virtual worlds in which they ostensibly cannot create game assets as we traditionally define them. Players are not able to create or modify creature models or change the code in an online game, but superstitions can create new experiences and social interactions for many players. For them, these superstitions are as much a part of their gameplay as the elements hardcoded by the developers. In a way, superstitions are free content for game developers; they are stories that require no additional resources or effort to create.

We tend to see superstitions as irrational, even primitive. And it's hard at first to see how ritual dances can be a good thing. But the key to every good story is engaging with the audience. A predictable story with no surprises is boring. The television and filmmaker J. J. Abrams refers to the use of a "mystery box" as a storytelling device to engage the audience as a story unfolds. Thus, in his monster movie *Super 8*, the audience never sees the monster until the last ten minutes of the movie. Until that point, the audience is actively engaged in guessing what the monster looks like based on the clues left in its destructive wake. And when the fans of TV show *Lost* were not watching the show, they spent a great deal of time thinking, talking, and posting on forums about the show's mysteries. Although superstitious rituals would be a bad thing in the jury room or the classroom,

I would argue that they are indicators of engagement in online games. Whether it's a story or a video game, nothing engages an audience like a mystery they can help solve. On the other hand, irrational behaviors are inherently hard to control. In chapter 5, we'll see how volatile beliefs have led to racial profiling in online games, but to understand how those beliefs emerged, I first need to explain why online games are so much work.

CHAPTER 4 THE LABOR OF FUN

Until I played *Star Wars Galaxies*, I never knew how absorbing industrial entrepreneurship could be.

The late afternoon sun was making me uncomfortable under the hooded robe and thick Wookie fur. The wild wheat field had been slowly depleted over the past week. Other surveyors had come and left their own automated harvesters—ugly metal installations that slowly blanketed the river delta. This wheat strain had a superior decay resistance, and I had frantically stockpiled it for my production of biological effect controllers. My pharmaceutical factories had ground to a halt three days ago owing to the break in the supply chain, but now, with this new wheat stock, I was hoping my luck was turning around. My clients were flooding the mail console, and if I couldn't deliver new stock soon, I would probably lose many of them to a competitor.

I turned to the sound of the approaching swoop speeder bike. It was that annoying donkey-faced Bothan again. I wondered if Laza ever slept. I had to planet-hop to find a new wheat source, and the quality was unlikely to match this wild strain. Perhaps a jump to Naboo first? I glanced at Laza, who was emptying his harvesters. I had a twenty-minute head start on him. I hopped on my own swoop speeder and headed toward the travel terminals. Earlier in my career, I had wanted to become a doctor, but the risk and adventure of pharmaceutical manufacturing certainly had its appeal.

Corellian Wheat

Yes, pharmaceutical manufacturing is a profession in a video game. We tend to think of video games as an escape from work, a mindless diversion. But just as superstitions find a way to flourish in virtual worlds, so, too, does work. As the technical capabilities of games increased, the complexities of play also increased. In 2003, two games launched that both had full-fledged player-driven economies: *Star Wars Galaxies* and *EVE Online*. In *Star Wars Galaxies*, which we will consider first, almost everything that was bought or sold in the game was created by another player. Apart from pharmaceutical manufacturers, players could specialize as tailors, architects, and even bio-engineers.[1]

The game captured the mundane minutiae of the manufacturing process from geological surveying to retail advertising. Not only did players have to assemble the components to create the final product, but there was a player who surveyed for the raw resources, a player who harvested the resources, a player who created the product prototypes, a player who used a factory to mass-produce the product, a player who developed the advertising, and a player who created the retail store to sell the product. The player population determined entirely the supply and demand of all these raw, intermediate, and finished goods. This round-the-clock commercial activity occurred in a public market called the Bazaar as well as through privately owned merchant droids spread throughout the galaxy. Truly dedicated players might try to manage an end-to-end production chain, but more often than not, informal cartels formed in which players could focus on a specific segment of the production chain.

The manufacturing process in *Star Wars Galaxies* was bewilderingly complex for players coming from hack-and-slash massively multiplayer online games. First, the quality of manufactured products depended on the quality of the raw resources used, and the galaxy was populated with a broad array of raw resources. For example, the biological effect controller (an intermediate component) required an organic component, which could be avian meat, berries, or wheat. The quality of the controller depended on the potential energy of the organic component. The math underlying manufacturing outcomes was sufficiently complex to warrant many player-written guides, littered with equations, such as:

$$\text{MAX\_EFFECTIVENESS} = ((\text{Resource1\_OQ} + \text{Resource2\_OQ}) / \text{COMBINED\_MAX\_OQ}) * 0.66 + ((\text{Resource1} + \text{Resource2\_PE}) / \text{COMBINED\_MAX\_PE}) * 0.33^2$$

Knowing what kinds of resources to seek out was only the first part of the problem. Locating high-quality resources required a lot of legwork. These raw resources were randomly located throughout planet surfaces in the galaxy. Once located through trial and error with the surveying skill, these resources could be harvested by hand or by setting down automated harvesters, which accumulated the resource slowly over time. Thus, early comers to a resource patch could take the most resource-rich spots, which yielded larger harvests. To resolve the problem of veteran players taking up all the rich deposit locations, every seven to ten days after a resource had appeared, the game would replace that resource with a randomly generated resource of the same class at a different location in the galaxy.

It was a never-ending game of musical chairs, and surveyors had to be on their toes to avoid breaks in their supply chains. Several third-party sites emerged specifically for players to input and collectively keep track of the emerging resources. Owing to the difficulty of maintaining high-quality resource stocks, many players made a living in the game merely from harvesting and selling raw resources.

Once players had located and harvested the resources, experimented with prototypes, and used factories to mass-produce the final products, they were faced with the biggest obstacle of all—each other. Because products had to be bought by other players, retail marketing was the true endgame. Successful entrepreneurs would often create a memorable brand name across their product offerings to create loyalty, especially important for their new product lines. Another strategy was to hire architects to design stylish and eye-catching stores to attract customers and enhance the shopping experience. Hiring exotic dancers also didn't hurt. Some players banded together to create centralized malls. And others took advantage of more devious tactics:

> I set about disrupting the sales of the other master weapon-smiths. I targeted one at a time. I would find out the location of their shops and set up a shop nearby. I'd pay players to loiter near the other weapon-smith's stores and point people over to my store with cheaper prices and I'd pay entertainers who were working in bars across the galaxy to advertise my store between sets. Finally, to really put the nail in their coffin, I'd pay a smuggler to use a special skill called weapon-splicing to improve my master-crafted weapons even more, thus giving my weapons the edge in quality as well as in price. [Star Wars Galaxies, male, 24]

Star Wars Galaxies created a living, breathing economy, and the hack-and-slash aspect of the game actually paled in comparison to the financial opportunities. Overwhelming an opponent in combat was one thing, but gaining the majority market share in a product segment while driving a competitor out of business certainly had its appeal.

Hadean Drive Yards

EVE Online, another online game with a player-driven economy, takes the work metaphor one step further. Player organizations in EVE Online are called corporations. Similar to the complex economy of Star Wars Galaxies, EVE Online players participate in a manufacturing-based economy within a dangerous war-torn galaxy. Resource-rich areas are constantly changing hands between factions depending on large-scale military outcomes. Furthermore, mining ships are under the constant threat of being hijacked by pirates and thus often hire mercenaries or have corporation members as bodyguards.

Hadean Drive Yards is one of many corporations in EVE Online. It sells manufactured starships as well as offering consulting services. On its corporate homepage located online (that is, not in EVE Online but outside the virtual world, actually on the Internet), part of their marketing material states that:

> Our R&D teams have done extensive research and testing over the course of time and have developed certain configurations which can be applied to your Corporate or Individual needs. Our ships are considered by many to be the most agile, mobile and hostile pieces of equipment in the Four Empires. While we do offer all the physical requirements to make, arm and deploy ships, we also offer our larger clients consultation services.[3]

Hadean Drive Yards has a typical corporate structure with executive roles and managers leading three departments: research and development, manufacture and production, and mining and transport.

The corporate hierarchy and chain of command are shown in an organizational chart available on its website. One of the roles in the executive branch is the human resources officer, who "handles most, if not all, of the hiring and firing and keeps up to date personnel files on all current and past employees." In an online recruitment post, the chief financial officer, Vladimir Tinakin, described the ideal applicant: "We're looking for bright and motivated capsuleers who are looking to belong to something bigger than themselves, and who want to find friendship as well as a knowledge of the game. . . . We have space for just about every play style." Apart from gaining access to new technologies, a benefit of joining Hadean is "mentorship which can provide insight and guidance towards your specific training curve." And you, too, can be a part of Hadean. Interested parties can find the application form at Hadean's main website. The application has twenty-two short questions and an essay question on the applicant's reason for joining Hadean. After submitting the application, the prospective employee is contacted and interviewed by a Human Resources representative. The recruitment post ends with this question: "Do you have what it takes to be Hadean?"[4]

In the same way that corporations evolved to take advantage of the free market, it makes sense that similar organizational structures have evolved in virtual worlds in which free markets are part of the system. Still, it bears pointing out that many gamers are becoming corporate cogs as entertainment. Some of these players review incoming applications and others set up interviews with the applicants. Online games are portrayed as fantasy worlds to escape work, but corporate work is now a form of digital play.

Dragon-Slaying

Slaying dragons is equally challenging work. After all, dealing with large teams of people, with varying personalities and motivations, is always difficult. The fact that you are interacting with orcs and elves doesn't make the people behind the avatars any easier to manage. The immature, self-centered player doesn't magically become wise and selfless when he or she types in a username and password. And yet, the rhetoric of dragons and swords doesn't only hide the work from outsiders, it actually makes it harder for the gamers themselves to see this work. The following experience by a *Guild Wars* player is actually quite common:

> Leading a guild is very rewarding, watching it grow and thrive, being respected by your members as a good leader. Politics and folks leaving the game eventually ruins the experience. Overall it was very fun, time consuming and an emotionally exhausting experience. Not sure if I would do it again. [*Guild Wars*, male, 41]

In the same way that dealing with other players was what made running a business difficult in *Star Wars Galaxies* and what makes cargo transport risky in *EVE Online*, other players make dragon-slaying difficult in games like *World of Warcraft*. Dragons do not have inner divas or bedtimes. People do. Slaying the dragon is actually quite straightforward once you've figured out how to manage a team of two dozen people to help you. And this is the crucial management problem that every successful guild leader must solve.

One of the main reasons to form a guild is to sustain a group of players to take on the team-based dungeons in the high-end game. For example, high-end dungeons in *World of Warcraft* require ten or twenty-five players. Although a solo player could certainly try to form an ad hoc team by shouting in the public city areas, many recruits will lose their patience while waiting for the team to form and leave. Dungeons also require specific combinations of combat roles, making it difficult to fill certain spots on the fly. And because these strangers have no loyalty to the group, the team often breaks up soon after its first failure in the dungeon. Guilds are a solution to both the availability and loyalty problems, at least in theory.

Sustaining a guild is no small feat. Sustaining a guild means making sure everyone in your guild is happy. Guild members who are unhappy quit the guild, or even worse, persuade other guild members to leave with them to form a new one. What makes managing a guild so difficult in online games is the wide variance in demographic background, life experiences, and motivations. In your guild is the hyper thirteen-year-old who is falling in love for the first time (and will soon be heartbroken for the first time), the college student panicking over what to major in, the stay-at-home-parent who is sleep deprived but so glad that the kids are finally in bed, and the war veteran who wants people to listen only to him. How do you make them all happy at the same time?

> God damn, people don't listen. I hated it. They are so whiny and expect you to do exactly what they say and give them what they want. Balancing the needs of 50 people suck. . . . I won't do it again. I don't even want to be an officer. Takes all the fun out of the game. [*World of Warcraft*, female, 26]

Think about the last time you had to work in a team of people (excluding family members) who were as young as ten and as old as seventy. Most people never have this experience in the physical world. In our daily lives at school or at work, we're often working with people of similar backgrounds. In college, we work on projects with other students, who are almost always within a three-year age difference. And companies generally hire people who fit the company culture and have specific kinds of educational training and skillsets. In online games, this social homogeneity is removed.

> The toughest part of being a guild leader is that my guild is comprised of people who have great personalities and get along really well, but are a real mixed bag of playing styles. You've got the guy who has 10 level 30 characters, you've got the guy who levels at a glacier pace, you've got the guy who hits 60 in a month but only wants to solo, you've got your hardcore raiders, the guy who has 8 level 60 toons, your casual players, your night crew and your stone cold PVPers. Trying to come up with goals and content for people like that, people who are all my friends, but have a million different goals, has been a really stressful balancing act. On top of which, I am a casual player who has a busy job and a RL of her own, and can't be on every night of the week to make sure everyone is happy. Being a guild leader has taught me about personality types and how to manage people more than any job I've ever worked on. [*World of Warcraft*, female, 27]

It goes without saying that being the perceived gatekeeper to happiness can be incredibly stressful. And it's a constant battle that always leads to disappointments.

> The most valuable thing I have learned from playing the role of a guild leader is one akin to life: No matter what you do there will always be some folks that do not like you. [*Legends of Cosrin*, male, 30]

Of course, your guild members are not only interacting with you. They're also busy gossiping, backstabbing, and getting fed up with each other. A common trigger for guild drama is rare loot—treasure dropped by monsters. Since five hours in a twenty-five-person dungeon yields only a few usable pieces of loot, tensions run very high when it comes time to determine who gets that loot. The following narrative comes from a female player who plays *EverQuest* with many offline friends.

Over time the more senior guild members and skilled players seemed to slowly begin leaving for one reason or another and the newer members kind of "took over." Eventually it all came to a head on one raid however, when a good friend of ours (also a senior member / officer) was put in a position of having to random roll on a piece of loot against a much newer member.

It ended up in a large debate, with people taking sides . . . one side believing that no one deserved loot more than anyone else regardless of time put into the guild, status, seniority, etc., and the other side angry that after all we had put into the guild we were being called "loot whores" for feeling that we deserved more than having to / random against some new member. The girl involved, her boyfriend (also a very good friend), myself, and my boyfriend left over this incident. I was very upset by the way the entire thing was blown out of proportion in the end and the fact that people I considered "friends" later stabbed me in the back with their accusations. [*EverQuest*, female, 40]

Guilds, with their mixed-bag personalities and competition for loot, are drama factories. Whether it's trivial bickering or a serious accusation, every time there is a conflict within the guild, as guild leader you are the go-to person who must decide what to do. To run twenty-five-person raids reliably, your guild needs to have between double to triple that number to ensure availability and plan for contingencies. In a guild of fifty or more people, interpersonal conflicts are constantly being escalated to guild officers and to you. And these conflicts are accumulating whether you are on- or offline.

The toughest thing about being a leader is people want you to solve their problems. You become their surrogate parent. It's analogous to running a business or any other organization in that respect. Actually helping them solve a problem or three is rewarding, but for me that pleasure is rapidly overwhelmed by the silliness of most of their problems. [*EVE Online*, male, 49]

Keep in mind also that high-end raids are pressure-cooker environments, with simmering tensions over past loot distribution and constant personality conflicts. Where there are limited resources, there is competition. To maintain control, guild leaders often devise rules and policies. And like office politics, resolving conflict in online games with a fair and firm hand while maintaining peace is challenging. It is difficult to be judge and friend at the same time.

A guild leader has to be den mother and bitch goddess in one. You have to be prepared to lay down the rules and abide by them, while at the same time, taking care of everyone in your guild. It's a lot of work and it's a really fine line to walk along at times. [*World of Warcraft*, female, 27]

It is hard enough to sustain a guild, but carrying out an actual raid brings its own unique set of challenges. First and foremost, you need to get ten or twenty-five people to show up at the same time. Since raids often run between two and six hours, you have to plan and schedule them in advance. The easiest way to do this is to establish a weekly raiding schedule that guild members can sign up for. Of course, getting twenty-five people to show up on time is another issue.

Getting everyone where they need to be, at the right time, is quite possibly the hardest part of a large-scale raid. There will always be latecomers, and not many on time. Making judgment calls—even when people are saying that they are incoming—on when to leave can be tricky. Leaving too soon will leave some people behind—and not likely give them a good impression of your raids (meaning they'll not likely go on another one of yours, and possibly speak out against raids you do). However, leaving too late will cause frustration to those that were actually on time, and want to get the event going. [*Ultima Online*, male, 18]

From the moment guild members start showing up, the raid leader is bombarded with unexpected events and must rapidly cycle through contingency plans. Billy signed up for the raid and told you he would come but still hasn't shown up after twenty minutes. Lisa, the primary warrior's girlfriend, is now asking if she can take Billy's place even though she didn't sign up. Steve wants to know if he has time to run to the corner store to buy smokes. The primary warrior is now also hassling you to let Lisa take Billy's place. Jamie is complaining that if the raid doesn't start soon, he'll have to quit early because he has the midnight shift tonight. You relent and let Lisa in the raid, and then Billy logs in the next minute. This level of crisis management is the norm, and the team hasn't even stepped foot in the dungeon yet. Once in the dungeon, your window of response time is much smaller. And you have to make those decisions under greater stress. After all, dragons will not wait while your team bickers.

> Then there are the contingency plans: What happens when things go south? Who is expendable (I played a wizard . . . trust me, it's wizards first—burn all you can before you go down to try to save the raid)? What happens when the primary tank goes linkdead? When do you suspend the raid and when do you charge on? And you have to deal with rewards: Who gets the loot and why? What if half your damage dealers go "brb . . . dinner" and, 20 minutes later, is still not back? [EverQuest, male, 29]

Defeating a raid boss is like stacking a human pyramid. Everyone has a role, and everyone must understand the bigger picture. If someone stumbles, they often take out multiple people with them. In World of Warcraft, Rotface is a patchwork monster (imagine a giant, bloated, misconfigured Frankenstein's monster) and is a moderately difficult boss. While the primary tank engages Rotface, smaller "ooze" creatures appear and begin attacking random raid members.

These oozes are strong enough to kill most raid members with a few hits, so the person being attacked needs to bring the small ooze to the secondary tank, who is running circles at the edge of the room. This secondary tank keeps the small oozes away from the rest of the raid. In the ten-person version of the fight, one healer is often assigned to each tank, while a third is assigned to heal the group. During this encounter, Rotface has a periodic slime spray attack in which he turns in a random direction and deals heavy damage to everyone in a cone area in front of him. Between the small oozes and the slime spray, all raid members need to be alert. If two team members accidentally stand in the spray area, the healers have to use mana that they could have saved. And when the healers can't keep up with the damage, raid members start dying and the pyramid starts to collapse. There are successful strategies to defeat every boss. But to succeed in a raid, team members have to accept and obey the commands of the raid leader.

> The hardest part is definitely to get people to listen to instructions from the raid leader. I'll take the most recent dragon raid I was at as an example. While running there after assembling the needed amount of players, the raid leader explained the rules of engagement on the way. And other participants commented on in other channels that he knew what he was talking about. One of the rules was to stay very, very close to the dragon, as it would otherwise be able to "single you out" if you ran a certain distance away from it, and would breathe fire on you, killing you and the people within a small radius of you. We get to the dragon and people seemed to forget quickly about that rule, especially "support classes" who apparently preferred to heal from a distance, thus getting killed first. [*Dark Age of Camelot*, male, 31]

In much the same way as football or basketball, explaining the strategy to a team is easy, but executing that strategy in the face of unexpected interferences is often challenging.

Of the things you expect to experience in a fantasy world, taking orders is probably not one of them. But in the same way that corporate structures emerged to take advantage of a free market in *EVE Online*, militaristic structures emerged in games like *World of Warcraft* to manage real-time, team-based combat.

> The most successful large raids tend to consist of experienced raiders who are completely focused on the task at hand, know exactly where to find the key information, and follow instructions without question during the active raid times. [*EverQuest*, female, 40]

In 2005, I interviewed Talon, who had been the leader of a high-end guild for three or four years. The guild began in *EverQuest* and was consistently the first guild on the server to kill many of the bosses. When the guild migrated to *World of Warcraft*, it was the first to kill Ragnaros (the last boss in the original game). In our interview, Talon isolated obedience and discipline as the most important factors in the success of a high-end guild.

> If I said something, people needed to do it instantly and they did. You never argued, especially on raids. Like I said, the organization was military style. To be successful you have to be organized. . . . If shit hits the fan, yes, they WILL follow the commands of the captain, but mostly because they know that if they don't act in a cohesive fashion, they will lose. In other words, the power is given democratically, but wielded in a dictatorial way.[5]

As you can imagine, these militarized guilds are not everyone's cup of tea, but succeeding in the high-end dungeons requires increasing amounts of centralized command, discipline, and obedience. The growing tensions from different guild factions wrangling over the goals and nature of the guild often cause guilds to split up.

A Second Job

These challenges of running a guild make it clear that being a guild leader is a lot of work. And more often than not, it is emotionally draining and cognitively demanding work. It is not something you would do to relax.

The toughest thing for me, about leading a guild was just showing up. I never wanted the job, but I felt obligated to maintain the guild I loved. I spent an average of 4 hours a day replying to ICQs and e-mails while attending alliance meetings in IRC [Internet Relay Chat] and writing up announcements for the website. This before I even logged in . . . which when I did, being a RP [role-playing] guild I was forced to attend every event and function I was invited to, to keep up community relations. Not to mention weekly guild and alliance meetings or any impromptu meetings that came up. Whatever time I had left was used up dealing with the inevitable daily guild issues. . . . So I got maybe one to two hours a week for myself. [*Ultima Online*, male, 35]

Given the player narratives we've seen so far on the challenges of managing a guild, it makes sense that some guild leaders would describe their gameplay explicitly as a second job.

After becoming a guild leader I found that I had taken on a second full time job. Creating a nice website was a pain and was time consuming. Then came trying to plan raids that the people in our guild could all attend (too much variation in levels), trying to keep people interested, recruiting new people. It was way too much work. [*EverQuest II*, male, 31]

The single toughest thing about running a guild is managing people. It can quickly turn into a serious job. You have to referee disputes, come up with events, loot rules, and organizational structure, recruiting. In short, running a guild is a lot of work, just like managing people in a real-life position. [*World of Warcraft*, male, 37]

Our society stereotypes games as places where no work gets done. And certainly, many gamers start playing just to relax after a long day's work. They want to kill monsters. They want adventure. But for many guild leaders, their digital escape becomes the very thing they are seeking to escape. The difference, of course, is that they aren't getting paychecks.

> Being a guild leader is a bit more responsibility than I enjoy in a game. If I wanted responsibility I wouldn't be hiding from the real world ;). It may also be that I work as a PR professional and being a guild leader feels a little bit too much like I'm at work. [*World of Warcraft*, male, 25]

> The toughest thing about being a guild leader is finding the middle ground between all the members, and being able to keep the group entertained at the same time. Being a guild leader is like being a manager at work, only without the paycheck. It's frustrating but rewarding to lead a group and see it function and grow, but it's a pain in the rear more often than not to get it to that point. [*EverQuest II*, male, 33]

Player motivations to achieve and socialize (as we saw in chapter 2) can inadvertently lead to tedious management roles. The deeper irony is that these guild leaders are paying around fifteen dollars a month for the "pleasure" of working a second job.

I've focused on guild leaders so far, but for a guild to function well and succeed in raids, everyone has to pitch in. In any given raid in *World of Warcraft*, ten or twenty-five people have all scheduled their lives to work on this one task for two to six hours every week. Since only a few pieces of usable loot drop, most of these players walk away from the raid with nothing but repair bills for their damaged armor. Given this net negative return and the social pressures of participating in raids once a player has joined a guild, many players in these situations also directly compare the game to work. The following pair of player narratives shows that this comparison holds true for players of all ages.

> But by the time I was level 50, the game was too focused on the "grind" to 60—the game required 20–40 players in raids—and the elitism, and classism of the players, just made it no fun. You could not achieve anything without massive support of some player group, and if you were in such a group (guild, etc.), they expected the game to be a full-time job. It was a burnout. [*World of Warcraft*, male, 53][6]

> When we became the max level, we participated in raids and joined a high-end guild. The game became a job. It lost that feeling we originally played for the raw fun, questing and exploring new areas, advancing characters. We noticed the game wasn't about that any more. It was only fueled by greedy intentions guild members possessed. [*World of Warcraft*, male, 18]

We made computers to work for us, but video games have come to demand that we work for them. Whether it is manufacturing pharmaceuticals in *Star Wars Galaxies*, running a corporation in *EVE Online*, or managing a guild in *World of Warcraft*, game play can become a second job. In the player narratives in this chapter, gamers have described their play with words including "grind," "pain," "stressful," "burnout," "obedience," and "discipline." These are hardly the words we would expect from consumers paying to be entertained in an immersive fantasy world. This is a prime demonstration of the Proteus Paradox; the offline burdens we thought we could leave behind follow us into virtual worlds.

The Blurring of Work and Play

In their book *Got Game*, John Beck and Mitchell Wade report survey data on the provocative differences between how gamers and nongamers think. They argue that gamers are more willing to take risks than nongamers because failure and repeated attempts are acceptable and expected in games. Beck and Wade argue that corporations will have to adapt to gamers, but perhaps not as much as they think. After all, the complexity and corporate metaphors turn modern online games into corporate-mentality training grounds. In online games, players manage, discipline, and overwork each other. It bears repeating that the average player spends twenty hours a week in an online game. And especially for younger gamers, these games may give them their first taste of being a cog in a large, structured organization that slowly burns them out.[7]

It's depressing to see grueling work in video games, but I wonder if we should be outright alarmed that we're now finding games in corporate work. The kind of adaptation that Beck and Wade foresaw is already happening. Jane McGonigal's *Reality Is Broken* and Byron Reeves and Leighton Read's *Total Engagement* are two recent books that champion the idea that games can improve engagement and empower workers, leading to increased autonomy and productivity. Both books also use online games as their pivot: If players can be motivated to accomplish complex tasks in *World of Warcraft* for free, can the same principles be applied to enhance corporate work or to improve our everyday lives?[8]

I have no doubt that games can be powerfully motivating, but the intentions of corporations are not always aligned with the well-being of their employees or the general public. If corporations provide a game that enhances worker loyalty and engagement, I wonder if these corporations will come to see their employees as being overcompensated. And more often than not, company policies do not benefit owners and employees equally. Health benefits are often sites of struggle. Health plans that employees prefer can cost the company more to provide, and I can imagine that companies would be interested in using games to help employees choose the "correct" health plans. Yes, games are fun, but games are also created by certain people to achieve specific goals. And in corporate settings, it is not the employees who are creating the games. For the time being, we don't have to be worried. Just as the technology research firm Gartner has predicted that the majority of corporations will use a gamified application by 2014, it has also predicted that 80 percent of gamified applications will fail because of poor design. But eventually, some companies will get it right.[9]

A fascinating aspect of many contemporary online communities is that they are able to incentivize people to perform work for free. Wikipedia—the collaborative online encyclopedia—is an obvious example. But also consider how Facebook generates revenue primarily by aggregating the information you freely share and allowing advertisers to target you more accurately for their products. Sociologist Tiziana Terranova has called this phenomenon "free labor." Games are uniquely powerful in converting paid work into free labor. Taken to its extreme, the premise of gamification is that any task, no matter how tedious, can be made engaging and motivating. And there is evidence that this premise is true. When unpaid laypeople solved the complex folding pattern of an HIV enzyme using an online game in 2011, it was heralded as a breakthrough in gamification. But this also means that game mechanisms can be used for less noble goals. Consider the possibility of a casual multiplayer word association game released by a marketing company in which the underlying goal is to generate high-impact keywords for marketing new products. Engagement and exploitation may be two sides of the same coin. When we receive these invitations to play, we must remember that fun can end up being a lot of work.[10]

The video begins with haunting electronica chords played against a black backdrop. As the lead vocals begin, the gameplay footage starts. The camera arcs around a gathered group of characters in a forest clearing, centered on a character named finalElf—the character recording this footage. The lead singer chants the word *karma* repeatedly as the video cuts to the gathered group rushing down the stairs of a stone fortress. They reach a large, open area of the fortress. finalElf approaches a female Elf from behind, pauses a second to adjust the camera angle for a better view, and then plunges a sword through her body. The female Elf slumps down on the stone floor. The lead singer shouts: "I said hallelujah." The camera zooms in on the scene as others from the group crowd around the corpse. The group heads into another area of the fortress, slaughtering characters along the way. The lead singer continues: "Come on and tell me what you need now. Tell me what is making you bleed." finalElf chases an elven archer through the halls. The archer suddenly stops and stands still, appearing to give up. finalElf shoots three arrows into the archer's back before he drops to the floor.

This massacre continues for another four minutes. The video, titled "Farm the Farmers Day," is the first in a series of five videos in which finalElf documents his group's systematic slaughter of Lineage II players suspected of being Chinese gold farmers.[1]

The Grind

In chapter 3, we explored superstitions in online games. I touched on the tedium of grinding, having to kill hundreds of monsters to gain another level. Although quests in the game provide experience points, they often bring players only partway to the next level. Players need to grind to accrue the remaining required experience points. The tedium of grinding is also exacerbated, as mentioned previously, because leveling-up time increases with each level. At the same time, quests get you less of the way to each next level. The result? More and more grinding is required to reach each successive level. In many cases, the quests themselves are just grinding in disguise. For example, a gang forces a local baker to pay a protection fee and would like you to kill ten gang members, computer-controlled enemies, in addition to the gang leader.

In 2005, I worked as a summer intern at the Palo Alto Research Center (PARC), where my colleagues had been running a data collection tool that took a census snapshot of several *World of Warcraft* servers every ten minutes. By the time I arrived at PARC, my colleagues had already collected several months of data. These snapshots included hundreds of thousands of characters, and the census data allowed us to calculate the average time it took for characters to reach each level. We estimated that it took the average player 372 hours to reach the maximum level in the game. To put this number into perspective, given that a normal workweek consists of 40 hours, that's more than two full months of workdays.[2]

For some players, the journey of leveling up is satisfying and pleasurable. Rather than a tedious grind, they find a relaxing activity.

> While there ARE things much more enriching and rewarding than mindless leveling, there's a certain . . . feeling of zen to be found in the grind. I've spent hours on end in the same area, doing the same thing over and over, watching the exp bar creep slowly upwards. Just soloing, just me and the monsters. [City of Heroes, female, 22]

But it is easy to see that grinding can become a chore for most players, especially if it takes two months to reach the advanced game. This is especially true for players who already work full-time and would be hard-pressed to devote much time to grinding. And for many players who make an hourly wage, an interesting calculus comes into play. Specifically, the ability to buy off large numbers of grinding hours with one hour of real-world work can become very attractive.

Guy4Game.com is one of many companies that provide power-leveling services. For a fee, the company's employees use the player's game account username and password to log in and grind through a certain number of levels in the game. When the power-leveling is complete, the service alerts the player via email. A typical cost in March 2013 for leveling a new *World of Warcraft* character to level 90 was $199, and the leveling up would take roughly seven days to complete. For players who make at least twenty dollars an hour and want a max-level character, the ability to trade one workday for months of grinding can be an incredibly attractive and sensible option.

Other players may enjoy the leveling process but might wish to speed things up a bit. Or they would like to reduce grinding without giving up control of their character. And some players might not wish to share their game password with a third party for security reasons. For all of these players, there is virtual currency to be purchased using real money. Virtual currency allows players to buy in-game weapons and items to kill monsters more quickly and thus level up faster.

A quick search on "wow gold" (the *World of Warcraft* in-game currency) using Google reveals dozens of websites offering virtual gold sales. The transaction is largely identical across these sites. Players identify the game and server their character is located on, and then specify the amount of virtual currency they are interested in buying. Most sites offer specific exchange rates (for example, twelve thousand gold for twenty dollars), with discounts for larger transactions. Players list one or more character names for virtual currency delivery and then pay for the virtual currency using a credit card or PayPal. Transactions are usually completed within a few hours. The seller will first try to deliver the virtual currency within the game world by messaging and meeting the player at a specific large city location that is easy to reach. The final transaction is then conducted using the in-game trade interface. If the player is not online when the transaction is made, the seller can send the virtual currency using the game's mail interface. The player can then retrieve the virtual currency from his or her mailbox at the next login. Because players cannot appeal these illicit purchases to the game companies in cases of fraud, the sellers' reputation is paramount and has likely increased the market share for the best-known and longest-running websites.

The prices of power-leveling services and virtual currencies hinge on the cost of labor. After all, it takes human labor to accrue both character levels and virtual gold. Because these online games are accessible globally, the market for these services is in reality a function of global economic inequalities. It wouldn't make much sense for a typical American player to pay another American player to accrue virtual currency because their wages are within the same order of magnitude. On the other hand, the lower cost of labor in developing countries makes such global transactions attractive. The act of collecting virtual currency is typically termed *gold farming*, and these players are called *gold farmers*. In 2007, technology journalist Julian Dibbell interviewed gold farmers working twelve-hour shifts in a fluorescent-lit office space in Nanjing, China. The game workers he interviewed in this "gaming workshop" were making 30 cents an hour and lived in dormitories adjoining the office spaces. Because of wage disparities between countries, therefore, an American player is able to trade a workday for many game grinding days. In short, these game services are a form of offshore outsourcing.[3]

It is difficult to get an accurate estimate of the size of this industry due to its shadowy and distributed nature. In 2008, Richard Heeks, an informatics researcher at the University of Manchester, published a report aggregating metrics from many sources. His estimates suggested an average wage for gold farmers in China of around $145 per month. Many of these gold farmers work twelve-hour shifts, seven days a week, which comes to about 43 cents an hour. On the demand side, both survey and game server data show that about 22 percent of Western players purchase virtual currencies. Heeks's best guess of the size of the gold farming industry is $500 million per year, and that it could well be more than $1 billion per year.[4]

The complex and repetitive nature of contemporary online games has created an entire industry in which some players are willing to pay someone else to play the game for them. And *World of Warcraft* has become a real place of work for these game workers. For them, playing *World of Warcraft* is an actual job. Or a sentence: the *Guardian* reported in 2011 that Chinese prisoners are being forced by prison bosses to "play" *World of Warcraft* at night to generate income, and so high-tech entertainment in the West has become a form of prison labor in China.[5]

Virtually Chinese

As the presence of gold farmers surged across online games in 2005 and 2006, gamers became increasingly frustrated with how these farmers behaved in the game. In particular, players have complained about three problems. First, gold farmers hog resource-rich areas, significantly increasing competition in those areas for normal players. Second, in order to drive normal players away from these resource-rich areas, gold farmers may employ hostile tactics, such as bringing monsters to attack the player or tricking unsuspecting players to engage in player-versus-player combat. Third, gold farmers are believed to ruin game economies by causing rapid inflation and increasing the supply of rare items to the point at which regular players cannot sell these rare items at a reasonable price.[6]

Even though gold farmers have been documented in Indonesia, India, Malaysia, Mexico, the Philippines, Romania, Russia, and South Korea, many academics and online gamers believe that almost all gold farmers are based in China. Heeks estimates that 80 to 85 percent of gold farming takes place in China but cautions that this is a "least worst" estimate based on the proportion of media and academic reports on the subject. I would add that there may be a self-fulfilling prophecy here of assumptions encouraging journalism and study in particular areas of the world, namely China. But even if that estimate is mildly or even moderately off, certainly many gold farmers are indeed based in China.[7]

Many gamers have posted their frustrations with gold farmers on forums and message boards. In the gaming community, many have used "Chinese" and "gold farmer" synonymously. On the official *World of Warcraft* forums, there was formerly a large message thread under the heading "Chinese people make me mad." The following post exemplifies the general sentiment in that thread: "He obviously was referring to the Chinese farmers. And I haven't heard of any group other than the Chinese that had operations set up to farm WOW gold and sell it for real cash."[8]

Even gamers who are shocked by the racial stereotyping are very aware of its existence in the community. In another thread titled, "Stop calling people chinese farmers!!!" a gamer commented on the overgeneralization and wrote that "it is just not nice." Other gamers responded with posts such as:

> They're all chinese and they all farm. case . . . freaking . . . closed.

> If something is a dog, you call it a dog. If something is a rose, you call it a rose. If something is a chinese farmer, you call it a chinese farmer.[9]

A French Canadian player recounts his encounter with an intolerant (and misinformed) player begging for gold. To rebuff the beggar, the player responded in French.

> So there is this guy: "can I get gold, I will send it back to you by mail, I want to buy an epic"
> Me: "pardon je ne parle pas anglais!"
> Him: "WTF hey do you have GOLD"
> Me: "Vraiment desole, je ne comprends pas!"
> Him: "I'll report you, f*** farmer, china FARMER are the suckx!"

Anthropologist Lisa Nakamura has documented how player-created movies, similar to the one I described at the beginning of this chapter, dehumanized Chinese gold farmers. They became second-class citizens in these online games. But dehumanization is a slippery slope. The hostility toward gold farmers grew to such a point that the rhetoric took a turn toward pestilence and extermination. In a post under the "Stop calling people chinese farmers" thread, one player defiantly replied: "I'll not only call them CHINESE FARMERS. . . . I'll call them a disease that has inflicted this game. Gold farmers are the rats of every game. They are everywhere and they multiply in a blink of an eye." Players expressed similar sentiments in my online surveys:

> The only good kind of farmer is a dead one. [*World of Warcraft*, male, 38]

> Yes. I enjoy killing gold farmers repeatedly. I play on PvP servers. [*World of Warcraft*, male, 26]

It was this toxic situation that produced the video documentary series "Farm the Farmers Day," discussed at the beginning of the chapter. These well-documented mob killings were the result. The perceived link between Chinese players and gold farmers, and the negative impact of gold farming on the economy, are all clearly stated at the end of the video:

> Farmers inflate the economy and prevent lower level players from leveling up. . . . As it is now people that are rich in real life end up being rich in the game, which is not right. . . . Ask NCSoft to ban Chinese IP addresses. They have their own server now, and do not need to be on ours to play. KS [kill-steal], kill, and harass farmers whenever you see them. Do not let them kill this game.

Even in a fantasy world of ogres and elves, your presumed real-life nationality can matter a great deal. Being labeled a "Chinese farmer" means you are fair game for systematic harassment and slaughter.[10]

As communication scholar Dean Chan has argued, Asian gamers are stuck between two entrenched stereotypes—the "model minority" and the "yellow peril." The case of gold farming perfectly illustrates how these stereotypes are intertwined. Suspected Chinese gold farmers are perceived as efficient workers, quietly and tirelessly gathering resources round the clock. But it is precisely this efficiency that has led to the pestilence rhetoric—their hard work is ruining the game. Thus, the anti-gold-farming videos leverage and perpetuate these historical stereotypes of the Chinese.[11]

Are You a Gold Farmer?

Chinese gold farmers do not walk around with signs above their heads advertising their illicit activities, so how exactly does one identify a gold farmer in a virtual world in which everyone is pretending to be someone else and where real-world ethnicities don't exist? The litmus test that some players use to make the determination reveals player biases in decision-making:

> I've encountered a lot of "probable" gold farmers in high-level zones. I tried speaking to them asking them to stop, if they answered in Chinese, I harassed them by luring mobs to them to interrupt their gameplay. If they speak English or any other non-Chinese language, I leave them alone.
>
> In Felwood, there was this annoying level 60 rogue that was farming all the Jadefire demons for felcloth. I asked her: "Are you farming for felcloth?" and she responded with 4–5 Chinese words. Since I was with my hunter, I aggroed about 3 other Jadefire demons, ran up to her, used Feign Death, and the 3 demons went up to her. [World of Warcraft, male, 24]

As I mentioned earlier, gold farmers hog resource-rich areas and this frustrates regular players, who also favor these areas. From a behavioral standpoint, then, a gold farmer and a regular player's activities look quite similar. They both stay for long periods of time, understand where monsters will spawn, and hunt those monsters efficiently. What the player narrative above reveals is that it is not the player's overt behavior per se that is damning but, rather, fluency in the English language. In other words, two players doing exactly the same thing at the same place at the same time are judged very differently depending on whether they are able to speak a few English phrases. The player that can speak English is left alone, and the player who cannot speak English is harassed.

Again, this demonstrates the assumed one-to-one relationship between two independent categories: Chinese players and gold farmers. If a person cannot speak English, he or she can only be Chinese and thus a gold farmer. Other players are troubled by this logic.

> I've never run into someone I assumed was a gold farmer, mostly because (unlike many people) I don't tend to assume that someone who doesn't speak English is automatically a gold farmer. I've seen people assume that because someone isn't a native English speaker and they see them playing for 8 hours straight they must be a gold farmer. Mind you, they know this person is playing there 8 hours straight why? Because they also are playing in the same general place for 8 hours straight. But because Player A used Chinese-inflected English they must be a gold farmer, because apparently Asians don't play games for fun. [/sarcasm] [*City of Heroes*, female, 36]

> I really feel though that about half of the people that are accused of being farmers are just people who cannot speak English that well. [*World of Warcraft*, male, 27]

Perceived resource-hogging is most apparent and frustrating to players who are themselves hogging resources. Often, a player who complains about a presumed gold farmer would like the resource the accused has gathered.

In 2006, an Australian businessman moved to Beijing for work and for a change of scenery. Being a *World of Warcraft* player, he wanted to continue his hobby even after the move to China. And since he was bored with his high-level male Night Elf hunter, he decided to create a new character—a female Dwarven hunter—on the same server. Wanting to mix a part of his new life in Beijing into his gaming, he gave this female Dwarf a Chinese name, Meiyuan. On his blog, he detailed Meiyuan's misfortunes:

> My wee yellow pig-tailed dwarf Meiyuan; body like a barrel, legs like tree trunks and the chest of a pocket battleship, she got called names. She has been insulted or players chat between themselves about Meiyuan in sometimes insulting ways. The general assumption seems to be that Meiyuan, actually me the player, am Chinese and that I am gold farming. Nothing to support any of this except apparent Chinese ethnicity because of the name.

Meiyuan was neither Chinese nor a gold farmer, but once other players assumed she was both, an interesting social dynamic emerged.

> There was one time I remember when I had fought my way through to an ore deposit. In the process, as I got to the ore, I saw that another player had also been embattled on the other side of the hill. I helped him out by assisting in the kill of his last opponent. I then turned to the ore. Since he too came to the ore deposit I had expected to share but the other player started calling me names, inter alia a gold farmer. His pals turned up, he again accused me of all sorts of things and his mates started name calling too. So I ignored him and emptied the ore deposit. I was there first and had first dibs and he apparently did not like that (and had no patience to find out if he got a turn or not—mouth first, thought second). Sod him.

Meiyuan was accused of being a Chinese gold farmer, and so Meiyuan behaved exactly how Chinese gold farmers are expected to behave. Meiyuan did not respond in English, remained mute, ignored threats, and continued to hog the resource. From the perspective of the accuser, Meiyuan was a Chinese gold farmer.[12]

Two English-speaking, Western players encounter each other in a virtual world. They have a disagreement, and one player accuses the other of being a Chinese gold farmer. The Australian businessman unwittingly becomes part of the Chinese gold farmer rhetoric and provides another concrete example of how Chinese gold farmers hog resources and need to be eradicated. We began this section by asking how players confidently identify someone as a Chinese gold farmer. One valid answer is that they don't. Chinese gold farmers and real-world ethnicities aren't simply identified in virtual worlds; Chinese gold farmers are created in virtual worlds and forced on characters to support a negative stereotype.

Gold Mountain

People came to this newly discovered land to become what they could not become elsewhere—heroes and millionaires. The early, undeveloped economy meant inconveniences. Certain mundane tasks required a great deal of time to complete. Many enterprising Chinese workers took advantage of the opportunity by providing a service that dramatically enhanced the quality of life. Providing this service required tedious repetition and painstaking attention to detail, and most of their waking hours were consumed by working in a small room in front of a machine. Nevertheless, their hard work did pay off. Some became wealthy, and the Chinese began to refer to this place as Gold Mountain. Yet their frugal industriousness incited others, particularly the Westerners who had arrived earlier. This triggered a period of systematic ethnic abuse and harassment. Individual Chinese workers were harassed and sometimes physically assaulted. Mob lynchings and massacres followed.

This story may sound incredibly familiar, but it did not take place in a game. I am describing the mid-nineteenth-century genesis of

Chinese laundry shops (*yi-shan-guan* in Chinese) during and after the California Gold Rush. Due to the perception of laundry as women's work and the scarcity of women in California during the Gold Rush era, the local cost for doing laundry was exorbitant. Miners, both white and Chinese, routinely shipped their laundry to Honolulu and even Hong Kong for cleaning and pressing. Even then, the price was high and the process took four months. As Iris Chang describes in *The Chinese in America*, Chinese entrepreneurs took advantage of this economic opportunity and created local laundry shops. This laundry work was neither easy nor glamorous; it was backbreaking work: "In time, the laundry became a humid prison. The typical washerman not only worked in his laundry but slept there at night. . . . On some days, a laundryman might labor twenty hours continuously, without even stopping to eat." But it was stable work that allowed Chinese workers to eke out a living in the United States.[13]

Chinese businesses—laundry shops, curio stores, and restaurants—multiplied quickly, but as the nation slid into depression in the 1870s, Chinese immigrants became scapegoats for a host of economic problems. They were accused of destroying the economy by working for less pay and by being pathologically frugal, and of draining the nation's wealth by sending wages to China. Newspapers and magazines portrayed Chinese immigrants as vermin and as consuming vermin as their main food source. Chang reproduces a magazine lithograph showing a dozen Chinese workers living in crammed rat-infested quarters, with two Chinese men in the foreground, squatting and feeding on rats. Anti-Chinese attitudes led in 1882 to the passage of the Chinese Exclusion Act. Instead of quelling anti-Chinese attitudes, the bill emboldened fanatics and led to a period of terror now called "the Driving Out." Chang reports that "several Chinese communities in the West were subjected to a level of violence that approached genocide."[14]

With both the Chinese laundry workers in the 1800s and today's Chinese gold farmers, workers identify and exploit an economic opportunity, providing a service to Westerners that improves their quality of living. However, complex economic problems are blamed on these immigrant workers, leading ultimately to genocide. What the 1800s story provides, crucially, is a rereading of gold farming not as a story of offshore outsourcing but as a story of immigrant labor—Chinese immigrants perceived to be encroaching on Western soil. At its heart, economic stress caused by inevitable resource competition is blamed on a vulnerable minority. As we saw earlier, resource hogging is something that many players engage in. What differentiates acceptable and unacceptable resource hogging is whether a player belongs to the in-group or the out-group.

The nineteenth-century history of Chinese in the West also highlights how complex economic outcomes can be pinned on vulnerable scapegoats. This is actually also true in the case of gold farming in online games. One common economic critique of gold farmers is that they ruin game economies by causing runaway inflation. This inflation in turn makes it incredibly difficult for low-level characters to succeed in the game. And indeed, inflation has been observed in many online games, which bolsters the argument against gold farmers. Yet the actual effect of gold farming on game economies is anything but obvious.[15]

When I was playing *World of Warcraft* in 2005, I noticed something odd about the game economy. The price of many goods in the market fell gradually over time. Large radiant shards, used as a reagent in enchanting, fell by about 50 percent within a few months. The same was true for crafted weapons and other player-produced goods. As Heeks has pointed out, this makes sense because gold farmers don't accumulate gold directly. Instead, they farm goods that are in high demand and sell the goods on the market to get gold. Assuming stable demand, the price on those goods will actually fall due to the increase in supply. In addition to keeping the cost of needed goods low, gold farmers might actually stabilize game economies by minimizing unpredictable shortage of goods. This is particularly true for hard-to-find components and items in the game.[16]

> In Lineage 2 they are everywhere, and everyone knows who they are. Initially, players were very hostile and attempted to harass them in large groups. After a while, players have realized that they are in fact necessary for the in-game economy to function properly and many of the farmers have become friendly with regular players. [Lineage 2, male, 22]

Heeks also points out that the effect of gold farmers is likely small in relation to the effect of normal players, simply because the majority of online gamers are not gold farmers. And because gold farmers are competing with normal players for resource-rich locations, gold farmers cause inflation only to the extent that normal players would abandon those resources if gold farmers left. Since normal players would exploit those same resources even in the absence of gold farmers, it's unclear whether gold farmers actually increase the in-game gold supply beyond what would otherwise have occurred.

What is more, game currency inflation has been a standard feature of virtual environments long before there were gold farmers, even back in text-based virtual worlds. Since monsters keep respawning and are an infinite source of in-game currency, inflation is guaranteed unless game designers create money sinks. It is only through money sinks that game currency can leave the system. For example, in World of Warcraft, players pay the game a set cost to purchase mounts (for example, horses and griffons). This currency then disappears from the game economy. But balancing virtual economies is a difficult task, subject to the interaction of hundreds of game variables and the actions of millions of players. Most game economies are inherently unbalanced and difficult to control. This also means that gold farmers are being blamed for economic problems that would exist even if they weren't present in the game.[17]

The gold-selling market in the West exists only because of the demand from Western players. In short, gold farmers are providing a service valued by a sizeable portion of the gaming community.

> I have no problem with gold farmers; I'm a professional and work full time, so my time is valuable, and they are providing a service. I've bought a total of about 5000g in WoW from an online website. I initially thought it was uncommon for people do to this, but the practice is actually very widespread, although people don't seem to like to talk about it. [World of Warcraft, male, 32]

> I have made it a habit of buying game-currency for real money, either from EBay or from www.ige.com (IGE). The reason for this is that making money in the game is a very slow and tedious process, and DAoC requires you to level up a crafter for the sole purpose of turning unusable loot into raw material, and then into trinkets that can be sold. . . . I spend $25 at IGE and can go back to enjoying the game rather than spend countless hours "working" (i.e. farming). [Dark Age of Camelot, male, 29]

In this sense, Western players are blaming Chinese workers for problems they themselves are creating.

We should also consider the role that game developers play in this story. After all, what we have is a form of entertainment that is so tedious and so repetitive that many people are willing to pay to not play the game. This is an artifact of game paradigms that reward time played rather than player skill—again a direct consequence of the deeply numerical leveling-up mechanics whose origins I described in chapter 1. You have to kill five hundred monsters to get to the next level no matter how competent or incompetent you are. Any player playing *World of Warcraft* can reach the highest level if he or she puts enough hours into the game. This game paradigm creates a powerful incentive to bypass the time sink. Instead of castigating the Chinese, we have to ask whether gold farming is simply a symptom of bad game design.

The Price of Cotton

Between 1882 and 1930, the price of cotton in the southern United States was directly correlated with the number of black lynchings. As economic conditions affecting the wealth of southern whites worsened, the frequency of mob violence against southern blacks increased. A more recent study of six central and eastern European countries has revealed similar correlations. In the mid-1990s, the perception of minority groups fluctuated according to economic conditions. Negative stereotypes of these minority groups increased when economic conditions deteriorated. These studies show that economic frustrations are most easily vented on a vulnerable minority group.[18]

As in the history of the Gold Rush, minority groups become most vulnerable when economic conditions are poor. Sudden surges of new players into an online game certainly lead to overcrowding of resource-rich areas. Players cannot always find or collect what they are seeking, especially since many game economies are inherently unbalanced and runaway inflation is difficult to control. It is also unfortunate that wealthy players are able to purchase in-game advantages. Players experiencing these economic frustrations may find it psychologically convenient and comforting to identify a scapegoat, blaming all the world's troubles on a vulnerable minority group that cannot even respond in English. And just like that, Chinese gold farmers become the singular cause of complex economic outcomes driven by diverse actors and variables.

Avatars are not created equal even if all are just made of pixels. And putting people in the same virtual world doesn't mean that they will all get along. More important, human beings always seek out otherness, whether online or offline. Things that shouldn't matter in virtual worlds matter a great deal—the color of your offline skin, the arbitrary national boundaries you were born into. The Proteus Paradox isn't only about how our psychological hardwiring doesn't change in virtual worlds, it's also about how our offline identities and ethnicities are forcibly dragged into online games in which national boundaries do not exist. In online games, racial scapegoating can lead to genocide. It means that simple insults, humiliation, and harassment of a minority group are no longer sufficient for venting frustration. The story of gold farming reveals again how our digital fantasies remain fully tethered to the physical world. How we play these games (and how some players can afford to not play these games) is very much tied to global economic differences and local labor costs. And as the histories of the American South and the California Gold Rush show, ethnicity can determine who to blame. Even in a world where humans and elves can coexist, a player's assumed offline ethnicity still matters.

CHAPTER 6   THE LOCKER ROOM UTOPIA

I've always been annoyed by the lack of a gender-neutral singular pronoun in English. In a plural context, you can resort to using "their," but in the singular form, you have to make do with the verbose "his or her" or the very situational and awkward "one." In Edward Castronova's book *Synthetic Worlds*, he avoids the verbose style and instead alternates with either "his" or "her" in his prose. And thus, in the section in which he argues that virtual worlds are a rational alternative for people living joyless lives in the physical world, he ends with the question: "If a person rejects a bad game in favor of a good one, who can blame her?" This question is ironic, not only because many gamers describe their game lives as being a stressful second job (as described in chapter 3), but also because the female pronoun highlights one of the most incongruent aspects of describing virtual worlds as utopias. In 2012, the Entertainment Software Association reported that 47 percent of all gamers are women. Whereas the video game industry demographics are approaching gender parity, the gender ratio in online games like *World of Warcraft* or *EverQuest* II remains highly skewed. Studies consistently show that only about 20 percent of players in these online games are women. If virtual worlds are indeed utopias, why are so few women playing these online games?[1]

One way that academics and game developers have addressed this disparity is to suggest that men and women prefer very different kinds of games. Under this logic, we just need to get better at understanding what these untapped female gaming desires are. This argument is often paired with an evolutionary psychology perspective. In 2000, the University of Copenhagen's Torben Grodal argued that men prefer action and shooter games because these games tap into men's evolutionary disposition to be hunters in a hunter-gatherer society; these shooter games dovetail with men's innate interest in developing spatial and motor skills for hunting. He concludes, "It is deplorable that the video game industry has not yet invented games that cater to those gatherer skills and motivations that are attractive to girls." Other researchers have echoed this sentiment. For example, Kristen Lucas and John Sherry identified several differences in gaming motivations between men and women and have noted that "redesign efforts [in games for women] should focus on playing into female players' natural cognitive abilities." Game designer Chris Crawford has taken this line of reasoning to its logical, albeit uncomfortable, conclusion: "All this leads to a suggestion for what might work for women in games: social reasoning. The ideal game for women, according to this simplified model, would be some sort of interactive soap opera or bodice ripper, presenting the player with complex social problems as she seeks the ideal mate." These arguments suggest that creating games for the "female brain" is the only sensible solution to attracting women to play video games; there is a set of feminine game mechanics we simply haven't found or perfected yet.[2]

As sociologist T. L. Taylor has argued, these attempts to create games specifically for women are "reifying imagined difference[s]" between male and female gamers. Because the assumption is that gameplay motivations are the primary barrier for potential female gamers, the women who currently play video games are perceived as "the oddballs, the nonmainstream, the exceptions"—they are aberrant women who can't tell us anything about real women. Certainly player motivation is an important variable, but trying to understand gaming by referencing brain evolution in the Pleistocene savannah ignores the reality of how people actually play games. Playing a game isn't simply about what players would like to do in the game; it's also about how they gain access to a game, their past experiences with games, who they play the game with, and how other players treat them once they are in the game. Gaming is an uneven terrain that presents different navigational challenges depending on the player.[3]

Boys Only. Do Not Enter.

Cybercafés are popular among Taiwanese online gamers because they offer decent computer equipment and convenience for friends playing together. They also tend to be seedy places filled with cigarette smoke and noise. Anthropologist Holin Lin has written about the social dynamics in these establishments. Most cybercafés locate the computer equipment toward the back, behind a room full of pool tables. Combined with the highly unbalanced gender ratio, it's obvious why most teenage girls would prefer to steer clear of the prying eyes and catcalling, and enter only if accompanied by a male friend. In short, Taiwanese cybercafés are male territories that women need male companionship to enter safely.[4]

The dramatic issues of physical access to online games in Taiwan actually mirror more nuanced issues of access for female gamers in the West. Even in the days of video game arcades, the degree of parental control and oversight exerted on boys and girls was different. Parents were more likely to restrict a girl's access to a video game arcade than they were a boy's access. The gendered territory of video games is made perfectly clear in other ways. In a census of video game characters, Dmitri Williams found that 85 percent of all video game characters are male. In fact, if you look only at the protagonists in video games, that number gets even higher: 89 percent have male protagonists. Female characters, when they appear, are typically relegated to secondary roles—sex objects or damsels to be saved. These social norms become a self-fulfilling prophecy. Boys encouraged to play video games grow up to become men who are interested in making video games. Girls, on the other hand, are discouraged from playing videos games and do not grow up with the desire to create these games. The end result is that video gaming is dominated by male game designers making games for male players. In Williams's interviews with game designers over a two-year period, he found almost no women. As he noted, "It is no surprise, then, that an industry-wide masculine culture has developed in which a male point of view is nearly the only point of view."[5]

The current dearth of women gamers is especially notable given the history of computer science. Before there were digital computers, roomfuls of human "computers" performed complex mathematical calculations by hand. Most of these human computers during World War II were women with degrees in mathematics. Compared with being on the battlefield, computing was perceived as women's work. When the first electronic general-purpose computer was built (the ENIAC at University of Pennsylvania during World

99

War II), the first computer programmers were drafted from this pool of human computers. Thus, the first six professional computer programmers were all female. Significant gender shifts in computing interest have occurred since then. The percentage of bachelor degrees in computer science awarded to women peaked in 1983–1984 at 37 percent. It has been falling steadily since: 27 percent in 1997–1998 and 12 percent in 2010–2011. When the first professional computer programmers were all women during World War II, and only 12 percent of computer science degrees were awarded to women in 2011, it is clear that social factors play a significant role in who does and does not engage with computer technology. The gendering of computing technology is a recent social phenomenon, and we shouldn't mistake the current disproportionate male presence in computer-related fields as reflecting an unchanging, innate, biological basis.[6]

These social factors have also created unspoken rules about who plays video games. In the same way that Taiwanese cybercafés are perceived to be male territories and accessible by women only when accompanied by men, the same is actually true of online games in the West. Data from the Daedalus Project have shown that a romantic partner introduced 27 percent of female players to online games, whereas only 1 percent of male players were introduced to an online game this way. And 60 percent of women in these online games regularly play with a romantic partner, compared with 15 percent of men. Many women in these games are also highly aware that male companionship is one of the few legitimate access points into online games.[7]

> I find that most people do not think female players in game are really female unless you have your significant other (husband, boyfriend, roommate) playing the game, too. I think most people in game assume

that 98% of all players are male and the other 2% are girlfriends / wives who were dragged along into the game—that it's not something a girl would want to do. [*World of Warcraft*, female, 38]

Many also seem to assume that I play with my boyfriend or husband, and are surprised when I tell them that I played MMOs long before my former boyfriend started playing City of Heroes, and that he doesn't play EverQuest at all. [*EverQuest*, female, 24]

Two threads of logic are revealed in these anecdotes. First, as games researchers Jennifer Jenson and Suzanne de Castell have noted, "for most women, transgressing gender norms in relation to playing games occurs most frequently when it is legitimized by male relations (boyfriends, cousins, brothers and fathers)." And second, a woman's biological sex is under question unless she can point to a male companion.[8]

But every once in a while, I seem to meet someone who wants to violently deny that I am who I am. And how am I supposed to respond to a charge of "You are not a girl!"—I can't exactly flash ID or body parts to prove it. [*World of Warcraft*, female, 36]

The assumption underlying this logic is that no woman actually wants to play online games. And this logic is rhetorically powerful; it legitimizes the presence of a woman in a male territory while preserving video games as a purely masculine pursuit. But for women, having to constantly justify your presence in online games quickly gets tiring. And if anything is a clear sign that you're not where you belong, it's when people question your body parts.

These issues of social access emerge not only when a woman logs on to a game but also the moment a woman walks into a gaming store. At an academic workshop at UCLA, I met Morgan Romine, a member of Frag Dolls, an all-female professional gaming group sponsored by Ubisoft. She recounted many experiences in which store clerks were shocked to realize that she was buying a video game for herself. When Romine was in Los Angeles that week, she stopped by the local game store to pick up a new Nintendo DS game. When she approached the counter, the cashier greeted her with, "So who are you getting this for?" She had a similar experience when she was preordering *Halo* 2. After the clerk chatted with her for a bit, it finally dawned on him that Romine was a gamer, and he blurted out, "Wait. You're ordering this for yourself?"[9]

Even when a female gamer's biological sex is no longer under question, other obstacles abound. Because women are often presumed to be uninterested in gaming, they are also often presumed to be incompetent gamers.

> I definitely classify myself as a gamer and make no bones about it to anyone. When I played EverQuest, I was so sick and tired of being treated like a moron or hit on 24–7 that I made a male character. The way people treat female chars and males in EverQuest was drastic; I had immediate respect. When on a female char, men think you don't know how to play, can't be hardcore, and try to give you things to hit on you. It's annoying to say the least. It's been this way in EVERY game I've played (EverQuest, Star Wars Galaxies, City of Heroes, and World of Warcraft). [*World of Warcraft*, female, 35]

And because women are presumed to be incompetent, their advice and insights are more likely to be ignored after their biological sex is revealed.

> I found that once people establish I'm really a female that some things I say get taken less seriously when it comes to strategy. [*EverQuest II*, female, 31]

> Once some of the people realized that I was female in real life, I noticed that a few of the members seemed less likely to listen when I made suggestions about how to manage certain fights, or which way to

go. Nothing terribly overt, but they would ask the group leader
instead, where previously they asked me. [*World of Warcraft*, female, 22]

Even in its most benevolent form, the underlying assumption of incompetence is apparent to many women.

Men in game are more likely to defend me with situations they'd just
let another guy friend handle. [*EverQuest II*, female, 31]

Playing an online game can be a struggle for women. If you say
you're a woman, few believe you. And if they do, you're now thought
of as incompetent, someone whose opinions don't matter and who
needs to be protected. For women who are experienced gamers, they
also recognize that any mistake they make will be assigned to their
gender rather than to circumstantial factors.

Even as gamers admit that some women play online games, these
women tend to be labeled "casual gamers." This euphemistic label
designates someone as having a passing fancy with online games,
and even though they are in an online game, they aren't a "real"
gamer. Again, this label acknowledges women are present in games
while simultaneously designating them as second-class citizens. A
study of *EverQuest II* players challenges this assumption. Server-side
game logs showed that women actually spent more hours each week
playing than men, by about four hours on average. But women were
more likely to underestimate their own playing time in the survey
compared with men. While men underestimated by about one hour
per week, women underestimated by about three hours per week.
And women were also less likely to indicate plans to quit the game
compared with men. The underestimation of playing time among
women highlights the power of stereotypes, and these data points
reveal the baffling irony of labeling the more frequent and loyal
players as being "casual."[10]

For many women, from the moment they step into a gaming store to when they log on to the game, they are bombarded with signals that they don't belong. They are presumed to have no inherent interest in games. They are presumed to be incompetent at games. And they are assigned labels, such as "casual gamers," that are disconnected from reality.

Male Fantasies

Because these fantasy online games are designed by male game developers to be consumed by male audiences, they are technologically constructed male fantasies in a very literal sense. And because this male point of view in the game industry is entrenched and largely unquestioned, the fetishistic aspects of these male fantasies have become largely invisible to male gamers. But they are very apparent to many women.

> Back in 1999, when I had recently gotten a computer and an Internet connection, I was standing in Wal-Mart, looking at the game titles. The two MMORPGs at the time were Asheron's Call and EverQuest. I read the back of both boxes, and both looked fun, but I picked Asheron's Call because the art on the box left more to be imagined. The figures could have been male or female. The EverQuest box (Kunark, at the time) showed Firiona Vie, with her blonde hair, impractical armor, and gratuitous cleavage, tied down, while an Iksar brandished a weapon at her. I read into that—this is what women amount to in this game: victims. [EverQuest II, female, 24]

This male fantasy is about both how women should look and what their roles should be. The sexually exaggerated design of female avatars is a common complaint of women gamers.

> The only really off-putting detail is that it's ludicrous that every time my elf fights, her breasts stick out to the side repeatedly. It is a constant

reminder to me that this game is made for 13 year old boys, or men who still think like them. [*World of Warcraft*, female, 42]

For the most part I completely agree with the generalization that video games are designed with the younger male in mind. It's very annoying to always see the same type of woman (hero or villain) who has giant breasts, large eyes and teeny tiny waists. [*City of Heroes*, female, 31]

The female players in these narratives make clear that female avatars are disturbing to them not only because of the sexual exaggeration but also because the avatars are a constant reminder that they have stumbled into some sort of digital peep show. As game designer Sheri Graner Ray puts it, female avatars are designed "as male players would like them to be—young, fertile, and always ready for sex."[11]

One common male defense to this argument is that male avatars are exaggerated, too, and thus that the unfair treatment is equal on both sides. Although it is true that male avatars are exaggerated, it is in a very different way. In female avatars, the exaggeration tends to be sexual in nature—large busts, low-cut clothing, sheer or almost non-existent pants. In male avatars, the exaggeration tends to center on strength or athleticism, not sexual features. Male avatars have unrealistically big muscles, yes, but we don't see male avatars with prominent bulges in their pants or tight stripper shorts that reveal the top quarter of their behinds, and most of their pants selections do not consist of briefs and thongs. In fact, as one female player noted, there is a very definite bulge problem in male avatars.

I find it somewhat disturbing that while the female avatars all have very prominent breasts, none of the male avatars have anything visible at the crotch at all. Their clothes are cut in a male style, but there's no "bulge" where things ought to be. If female avatars are made to approach some "ideally attractive" or "sex-specific" model, then male avatars ought to be the same, rather than being de-sexed. [*World of Warcraft*, female, 31]

Thus, even though both male and female avatars are distorted, very different features are being exaggerated. And if you are a heterosexual male gamer who is made even the slightest bit uncomfortable reading about prominent male bulges in thongs, then perhaps that gives a hint of what women gamers feel when they play a female avatar in most online games.

The sexualized female avatars also encourage sexual harassment. The immediate visual of a scantily clad, voluptuous female is the only point of reference available in the game of who another person is and makes it easy to attract unwanted attention.

> One thing that pushes many women away (or in my case into playing a male character) is the ogling and cat-calls that can go on in games. I was astounded that people would hit on a cartoon in a lewd manner. [*EverQuest II*, female, 42]

Sexual harassment is something that many male players experience for the first time when they play a character of the opposite gender in an online game.

> I never realized how irritating it can be to have to put up with unwanted advances. [*EverQuest*, male, 38]

> I'm amazed how thoughtless some people can be, how amazingly inept men are at flirting and starting a conversation with a female, and how it really does take more effort to be taken seriously as a female versus a male. [*EverQuest*, male, 24]

The same piece of armor often looks different when it is worn by a male avatar compared with when it is worn by a female avatar. Not only is the armor tailored differently for the different body silhouettes, but in the case of many high-level or rare pieces of armor, the cutting and design may be entirely different as well. More often than not, male armor pieces tend to cover the body, whereas female armor pieces tend to reveal the body. Oddly, this differentiation tends to intensify with the increased rarity or higher level of the armor. On the official forums for *Diablo III*, one female gamer articulates her concern over her high-level wizard armor:

> I realize this is a controversial topic among many gamers—particularly male gamers who want female characters to look like prostitutes regardless of how the women who play them feel—but I've come here to post about the level 63 pants on a female wizard. . . . The pants are "crotchless" and have no thighs to them; they're essentially high-riding underwear with no pant around them but on the outer legs. I think I'd prefer just to wear underwear at that point. . . . I want to be a wizard, not a pornstar. . . . I don't even really mind the highly impractical stilettos on my demon hunter or the crazy cleavage on some of her cloaks, but Archon Faulds are just ridiculous sex shop attire.[12]

Although this asymmetrical design has been in place for more than a decade—it has almost become an inside joke among gamers—there is an insidious logic embedded in this asymmetrical armor progression. As male characters level up and become more powerful, their bodies become better protected and covered. In contrast, as female characters level up and become more powerful, their bodies are uncovered and made more vulnerable. Thus, as women gain power, they are disempowered in another way. Unfortunately, this is the only logical endpoint of a male fantasy that uses female bodies as sexual objects to be controlled. Whether it is Firiona Vie chained and held at swordpoint or a powerful female wizard in crotchless pants—two visual references that bookend roughly twelve years of online games—the message is that all women, no matter how successful, are vulnerable sexual objects.

Perhaps the greatest irony of this male fantasy is that women are simultaneously highly desired and shunned. Idealized female body parts are put on display and ogled, but the moment a real woman steps into an online game, her presence is deemed suspect and her body parts are questioned. Women are worshipped and idolized as long as they are not real; it is in this sense that online games reveal their function as a male fantasy. And perhaps another reason why games deny women access is because the male fantasy can be sustained only by presuming a male audience.

A Wrinkle in the Numbers

One caveat in this male territory discussion is that studies have consistently identified statistical differences between male and female gamers. In particular, many studies have found that women are less interested in the achievement and competitive aspects of games than men are. And in the interest of full disclosure, I've found and reported these findings in my own research. These data seem to suggest that a gender partitioning of games or game genres is sensible. But there's actually a wrinkle in these data.[13]

In psychological research, two samples are "significantly" different from each other if the difference between them is greater than chance alone would predict. In psychology journal papers (and those in related social science fields using quantitative methods), the term *significant* is reserved for this statistical meaning; however, whether the difference is substantively meaningful is an entirely different issue. This is because the ability to detect differences is a direct function of the number of participants in a study. In studies with large samples, even very small differences can become statistically different. For example, in one survey of over a thousand *World of Warcraft* players, I found a statistically significant difference between players of the two factions—players who prefer Horde were on average 27.5

years old, whereas players who prefer Alliance were on average 28.7 years old—but this marginal age difference isn't very meaningful. Thus, you might have a statistically significant difference that is substantively trivial.[14]

We can also turn the statistics of difference on their head and instead calculate the statistics of similarity. In my own data on gameplay motivations, the largest difference was found in the mechanics motivation (that is, rules and optimization), but even here the overlap between men and women was 67 percent. The average gender overlap across all the gaming motivations listed in chapter 2 was 82 percent. The findings from another study of EverQuest II players show a similar pattern. Even though the difference in terms of how strongly men and women were motivated by achievement in online games was significant, the overlap was 70 percent. What these numbers show, when we look at statistical *overlap* instead of statistical *difference*, is that the majority of male and female players in online games actually like the same kinds of play. In fact, psychologist Janet Shibley Hyde has found this same pattern of gender similarity across a broad range of psychological variables outside of game-playing. When we look at gender similarities instead of gender differences, we find that claims of dramatic differences between men and women are often inflated. Attempting to identify gaming motivations that appeal to the "female brain" might be attempting to solve a problem that doesn't really exist.[15]

Not only are the gender overlaps large, but the gender differences are actually inflated at the outset. One danger of studying gaming populations (or any natural community) is that of bringing underlying biases into the data. The gender difference in achievement motivations is a good case in point. It turns out that age influences the achievement motivation more than gender; older players are much less interested in goals and competition in online games compared with younger players. In fact, the relation between age and the achievement motivation dwarfs the gender difference. Age explains almost twice the statistical variance in this motivation compared to gender. It also turns out that, on average, women in online games are older than men by almost six years. Thus, when researchers compare the superficial gender difference without factoring in the age difference between men and women, they exaggerate the observed difference in the achievement motivation.[16]

Moreover, women gamers are perfectly capable of saying what they want and don't want in a game.

> I think that by marketing specific games for women, game companies are patronizing women and missing the point of the problem entirely. They don't need to make games specifically for women (games which usually involve shopping, or other stereotypically feminine things). They need to make current games less sexist so more women will be interested in playing them. Lots of women enjoy MMOs, FPSs [first-person shooters], and other popular kinds of games. But when these games give them the message that women are best when they're all T&A [tits and ass] all the time, they are not appealing. [*World of Warcraft*, female, 27]

> There isn't really a concept of a "game for boys": men I know play everything from Japanese RPGs to tactical simulations to FPSs, yet women are expected to ALL play The Sims, as if there aren't just as wide a variety of tastes amongst women as there are amongst men. [*Dungeons and Dragons Online*, female, 26]

As we've seen here, although there are numbers that show gender differences in gaming motivations, these statistical differences are often not as straightforward as they may appear.

Gender-Bending and Gendered Bodies

We've seen how gender expectations are encoded into and sustained as male technological fantasies in both the design of avatars and the powerful rhetoric, which allow women into these spaces but as second-class citizens and sex objects. By allowing players to have fluid bodies, virtual worlds actually go one step further. These online games are uniquely powerful tools for perpetuating stereotypes.

On its surface, gender-bending seems like the perfect counterpoint to my argument that these games provide a false freedom. At the click of a button, men and women can switch their biological sex and experience life from an entirely different perspective. What could be more liberating than that? Indeed, among *World of Warcraft* players, 29 percent of men report having a main character that is female. On the other hand, only 8 percent of women report a main character that is male. When looking across all the characters that a player has, the same pattern remains. Fifty-three percent of men have at least one character that is female, whereas only 19 percent of women have at least one male character. On average, 33.4 percent of men's characters are female, whereas only 9 percent of women's characters are male. No matter how we slice it, men gender-bend roughly three to four times more often than women. On the Daedalus Project, my post on this gender disparity in gender-bending has elicited more than two hundred comments from players trying to explain this phenomenon. By far, the most widely adopted male explanation is that the third-person perspective in these games means that players spent a great deal of time looking at the back of their character. As one male player put it, "If I am going to stare at a butt all game it might as well be a butt I'd like to look at." Data my colleagues and I gathered at the Palo Alto Research Center provide empirical support for this. When men gender-bend in *World of Warcraft*, they tend to play races with attractive female characters: Humans, the Draenei, and Blood Elves. Races with unattractive females—the diminutive dwarves or the giant, muscular, cowlike Tauren—are seldom selected by men who gender-bend. In short, gender-bending among men is often an artifact of the sexualized female avatars, rather than an explicit attempt to explore gender roles.[17]

Virtual worlds also allow false gender stereotypes to be made true. In a study of *World of Warcraft* players in which my team combined survey data with in-game log data, we first asked players whether they thought male or female players preferred certain activities in the game. These included different combat roles, such as healing, tanking, and damage-dealing classes, as well as noncombat activities such as crafting. The most strongly stereotyped female game activity by far was healing; players believed that women have a much stronger preference for healing compared with men. We found that this was not the case. We calculated the ratio of total healing output compared with total damage output for each player in the study. This healing ratio allowed us to get around the noise of some players playing more hours a week than other players and get to a comparable measure of healing preference. We found that male and female players had almost exactly the same healing ratios—33 percent for men, and 30 percent for women. Thus, the stereotype that women prefer to heal in online games is false. Men and women have the same preferences for healing.

Where we did find a statistical difference was in *character* gender. Female characters had a much higher healing ratio compared with male characters. This disparity was a direct consequence of how players behave when they gender-bend. When men gender-bend and play female characters, they spend more time healing. And when women gender-bend and play male characters, they spend less time healing. In other words, when players in *World of Warcraft* gender-bend, they enact the expected gender roles of their characters. As players conform to gender stereotypes, what was false becomes true. Thus, when players interact in the game, they experience a world in which women prefer to heal.[18]

Jesse Fox, a communication scholar at the Ohio State University, has found that the design of female avatars can elicit dangerous stereotypes. In her study, students were put into a virtual world and interacted with a variety of female avatars. She found that female avatars that conformed to gender stereotypes—a coy, conservatively dressed women or a dominant, suggestively dressed women—increased sexist beliefs and rape myth acceptance. In short, participants exposed to scantily clad female avatars were more likely to believe that women who get raped deserve it because of their perceived promiscuity. In virtual worlds, false stereotypes are being made true via play.[19]

Rethinking Utopias

The things we build often become contaminated with unspoken preconceptions and prejudices, whether this is a technological artifact or something as mundane as a road:

> Anyone who has traveled the highways of America and has become used to the normal height of overpasses may well find something a little odd about some of the bridges over the parkways on Long Island, New York. Many of the overpasses are extraordinarily low, having as little as nine feet of clearance at the curb. Even those who happened to notice this structural peculiarity would not be inclined to attach any special meaning to it. In our accustomed way of looking at things like

roads and bridges we see the details of form as innocuous, and seldom give them a second thought.

The highway developer Robert Moses designed these low overpasses for the same reason that he vetoed a proposed railroad to Long Island: his decisions ensured that the twelve-foot-high buses used by the lower class would be unable to navigate the parkways, reserving Long Island's beaches for white, privileged New Yorkers. Political theorist Langdon Winner argues that human artifacts embody politics—the things we build can implicitly regulate who does and does not belong.[20]

The fantasy worlds we build also have these unspoken rules. From the moment a woman steps into a gaming store or enters an online game, she receives cues that she doesn't belong. Virtual worlds and online games are crafted by people with certain mindsets and biases that are too often hidden and unquestioned. As with the color of our skin or the national boundaries we happen to fall into, our offline biological sex still matters in virtual worlds. In this instance of the Proteus Paradox, false beliefs and stereotypes of women are not only being perpetuated in virtual worlds, they are being made true via play.

I've focused on online games in this chapter, but sexism isn't a gaming problem; it's a social problem. Although having more female game designers would likely lead to more gender-inclusive games, the dramatic statistics on awarded degrees in the computer sciences illustrate that as a society we have very different expectations of what careers men and women should pursue. In addition to career stereotypes, there are also striking differences in how men and women think of their free time. Studies have consistently shown that women have less free time and that their free time is more likely to be infringed on by gendered expectations of housework and child care.

Because these gender-stereotyped household responsibilities (some ever-present, others unpredictable) are co-located with leisure spaces in the home, women often feel less relaxed and more pressured even when they are ostensibly free. Thus, women are more likely to experience guilt when they engage in leisure activities in the home. This conflicted sense of leisure is exploited quite effectively by advertisers. From body lotion to chocolates, from yogurt to spa treatments, products are often marketed to women as guilt-free indulgences— that just this once, they can indulge in something special without feeling guilty about it. Advertisements for men almost never employ guilt. But this trope reveals an important social message: women are normally expected to feel guilty about leisure and pleasure. The stereotype of gaming as a waste of time likely exacerbates this expected guilt and further lowers women's desire to game.[21]

Sexism isn't a conspiracy that men carry out against women; it's how we as a society treat men and women differently and shape how they should behave. It limits the life choices of both men and women, and it is sustained by both men and women. The Difference Engine Initiative was a 2011 Toronto-based workshop that tried to support women entering the indie game community. The female president of the initiative, while acknowledging that clients often wanted to talk to her male colleagues rather than her, disagreed that gender was a significant barrier to success in the industry. Instead, she told participants to develop a thicker skin. A human resources executive from Electronic Arts makes a similarly conflicted argument in an opinion piece in Forbes. Gabrielle Toledano writes, "The problem isn't sexism. . . . Sexism is an unfortunate reality of our times, but as women we must seek the power and ability in ourselves to change the dynamic." But arguing that women need to work much harder simply because they are women only reinforces the sexism that both female executives claim isn't a problem. The last time I checked, no one is telling boys that they need to try much harder to enjoy video games. Sexism in gaming is a symptom of a much larger social problem. Its roots are deep and widespread. This is why it's such a difficult problem to fix.[22]

CHAPTER 7

THE "IMPOSSIBLE" ROMANCE

> I was approached by a somewhat rude gnome who was making some
> rather rude remarks to me, and this lovely paladin (they're always
> paladins . . .) came to my rescue and scared off the gnome. Then he
> bought my character some pinot noir and we chatted for awhile.
>
> [*World of Warcraft*, female, 23]

For the past few chapters, we've seen how our psychological baggage
and offline politics can carry over into virtual worlds. But having
reality intrude into virtual worlds isn't always a bad thing. In this
chapter on romantic relationships, I'll describe one example of how
the Proteus Paradox can be beneficial. In an online game, how do
you get to know someone when he or she is hiding behind the avatar
of an elven assassin or undead necromancer? The stunning graphics
of today's online games make it easy to forget that people have been
creating their own digital personas for more than three decades, well
before graphics cards were a standard feature in personal computers.
Even in early text-based virtual worlds and online communities,
users could reinvent their identities. One striking story from that era
still resonates with how we think about online relationships.

In the early 1980s, when the Internet was still in its infancy and
restricted to military and educational use, tech-savvy people could
interact online via modem networks. CompuServe operated one of
these networks in which people could pay an hourly fee to dial in via
their modem to access many services, from stock quotes to weather

reports to airline information. There were also social channels on which users could mingle, which allowed users to chat in large groups as well as one-on-one.

In 1983, a woman named Joan gained celebrity status on one of CompuServe's social channels. Joan, a neuropsychologist in her late twenties living in New York, was the victim of a drunk-driving accident that killed her boyfriend and left her severely disfigured, mute, confined to a wheelchair, and suffering intense pains in her leg and back. In the ensuing depression, Joan had frequent suicidal thoughts. But her life turned around when a former professor introduced her to CompuServe, where Joan's physical disabilities no longer mattered and she was able to express herself and develop friendships.

Joan became an inspiring presence on CompuServe. She developed close relationships with many women who called each other "sisters." Everyone who knew her described her as being extraordinarily generous. When one of her friends became confined to bed rest due to a disability, Joan bought her a laptop. When the same friend mentioned that no one had ever sent her roses, Joan sent her two dozen. And despite her physical limitations, Joan tried to resume her teaching career by using typed lectures displayed on large screens. She worked with a police task force to crack down on drunk drivers. On one of these projects, she met a police officer named Jack Carr. They fell in love, got married, and honeymooned in Cyprus.

But then it all slowly began to unravel. Some of Joan's friends, particularly those with physical disabilities themselves, found her stories far-fetched. They doubted that Jack Carr even existed but took pity on Joan's way of dealing with her own tragic situation. And although Joan's muteness and disfigurement were at first legitimate reasons for why she didn't want to speak on the phone or meet in person, this reticence didn't align with her amazing stories of traveling to conferences and honeymooning in Cyprus. Slowly, it dawned on Joan's online friends that none of them had ever seen Joan in person in all the years that they knew her. One of them finally confronted Joan with these doubts. Joan wasn't actually a neuropsychologist. Joan wasn't in her late twenties. Joan wasn't even a woman. "Joan" was a male psychiatrist named Alex in his early fifties who had created a female persona to understand how to interact with his female clients. The public outrage was swift and brutal. One of Joan's friends called Alex's deception "mind rape."[1]

Stories like this have become cautionary tales for meeting someone online, particularly when it comes to romantic relationships. It is difficult to find studies of attitudes toward online gaming relationships specifically, but in a 2006 survey conducted by Pew Internet on online dating, 43 percent of respondents agreed that this activity involves risk, 57 percent agreed that a lot of people online lie about their marital status, and 29 percent agreed that people who use online dating are desperate. Nevertheless, sociologist Michael Rosenfeld has found that between 2007 and 2009, 21 percent of the heterosexual romantic relationships formed in the United States began online; for same-sex couples, it was 61 percent. But finding love in an online game is a different matter. Yon is a thirty-eight-year-old gamer who recently emailed me. He met his wife in an online game when he lived in the United States and his wife lived in the United Kingdom. They managed to make their relationship work, and they now have two children. Nevertheless, he notes, "This often makes for an embarrassing moment when people ask how we met. . . . The stigma of being a gamer and meeting online is still a strange concept to some." In one of her interviews with online gamers, sociologist T. L. Taylor finds this same stigma. Kim met her husband in the game EverQuest, but this is "something she does not tell too many people." Given the stories of deceptive online relationships and the way gamers censor their own successful relationships, it's not hard to see why many people have concerns about finding love in an online game.[2]

In my survey studies, I have found that a good number of people have physically dated someone they first met in an online game. About 30 percent of online gamers have had romantic feelings for another player, and between 9 and 12 percent of players have physically dated someone they first met in an online game. To learn more about how these relationships started and how they progressed, in 2006 I asked players to describe the trajectory of these relationships. The 115 respondents to the survey were all players who had physically dated someone they had met in an online game. One data point jumped out at me: 60 percent of the players didn't think they would have dated their significant other if they had first met face-to-face.[3]

Sketches of Love

In the survey, players walked through their love stories—how they met, how they fell in love, how they decided to meet face-to-face, and how it all turned out in the end. As I read through the hundred-plus player narratives, a common pattern became apparent.

Let's start at the beginning of the archetypal love story, the moment players met their future romantic partners. Overall, these initial meetings happened in very mundane and common situations, and the chemistry was seldom immediately apparent. In none of the stories did any player say it was love at first sight.

Our characters met in North Freeport in EverQuest. His dark elf cleric was on top of the roofs, an area which I didn't know characters could access. I sent him a /tell, asking how he got up there, and he kindly showed me how. [EverQuest, female, 22]

My fiancé and I met in EverQuest in mid-1999. It was a totally by accident moment. I was a low-level Bard fleeing the bandit camp in North Ro after a bad group pull. I was barely alive and in the Oasis of Marr. I nearly ran over my fiancé's character sitting on a dune. He looked low level (that was the fate of wood elf druids for soooo long) so I chatted with him a bit. Boy was I surprised when all this healing and buffing came from a low-level player. I thanked him greatly and since he was nice I added him to my friends list. [EverQuest, female, 35]

In many cases, both players belonged to the same guild. This made it easy for repeated encounters to occur, and the guild also provided a convenient context for chatting and grouping with each other. Instead of having to create a contrived situation to talk to someone, being in the same guild offered a wide variety of acceptable openers. This could be getting help for a quest, getting advice on equipment, planning a future group quest, or telling a story about something that happened earlier.

I was aware of her character in a vague way as "the competition" when we were both in different guilds (we were both Celt Wardens in Dark Age of Camelot). Then she quit her guild, and joined mine. We played at different times, but people kept saying things like "lol that's just what [she] said!" about things I said, and apparently vice-versa, so we started to take note of each other, as we had both thought we were pretty unique. [Dark Age of Camelot, male, 28]

Met her when she joined our guild. Once I stopped playing that game (Dark Age of Camelot) and she took on the role of guild leader, I remained as an advisor. It wasn't until after we both left that game (but stayed in the same guild) that we became romantically involved. [EverQuest II, male, 32][4]

The romantic tensions in these casual relationships then slowly build up in an incubation period. As these players work with each other in groups and chat during downtime, they begin to wonder if there's something there. Among the player narratives, this period seemed to run anywhere between two weeks to twelve months.

> We started to get to know each other out of character and became friends, chatting about our day and about life in general. After a couple months of this, I went through a period when I was having a very rough time at work. He was very sweet and considerate to me through that time, asking how I was and listening to me bitch about things. [World of Warcraft, female, 30]

> We started out as two people who were looking for a group. None were available, so we decided to group together. Upon doing so, we discovered that we enjoyed the conversation. We decided to make it a nightly event. It had been a few weeks of spending 6 hours a night together and then one of us had to take a break for several days. When the two of us were reunited in game, it was different. It was awkward, I believe, because we both figured out that we missed one another. [EverQuest, male, 25]

Often, these romantic feelings then grow to a point at which one player finally decides to express his or her feelings for the other person. The uncertainty of reciprocation heightens the tension and anticipation of the moment of truth, much as it would in a face-to-face relationship. Most players had fairly detailed descriptions of this turning point of their relationship. This first narrative continues from the same player we just heard from above.

> We talked about it the same way we talked about everything else, in game. We were chatting and it came up. We talked about our feelings and what it meant for our current situations, and we were both giddy. The moment was like . . . beyond words. Let us say that. [EverQuest, male, 25]

About 6 months into World of Warcraft I met someone who lived in the same state as I and was planning to meet him. My now boyfriend then said "I don't want you to meet him. I have feelings for you." I had had feelings for him all along but was too afraid to say anything. When he told me he wanted to be with me I was on cloud nine. I couldn't believe it but was so happy that he felt the same way. [*World of Warcraft*, female, 29]

Following these declarations of affection, the couples begin to take advantage of other communication mediums. These often include instant messages, emails, phone calls, and webcam chats. Contrary to the idea that people rely solely on typed chat to develop their romantic relationship, players use a variety of communication tools to better understand their romantic partners. Players don't simply jump from avatar to meeting face-to-face.

Hunting together built an in-game friendship, server downtime and wanting to dissect the night's play more privately than in-game led to chatting over an IM [instant messaging] program. Chatting outside the game led to friendship in our non-gaming life, which eventually developed into a flirtation. He had a web cam so I was able to see him from time to time and watch his mouth move out of synch with what he was typing. [*EverQuest*, female, 34]

After many many hours of in-game playing and some role playing together we seemed to have a good feel for each other's personalities irl [in real life]. We exchanged IM's and Phone# and chatted a lot. Then came photos and some webcams. [*World of Warcraft*, male, 24]

During those four months apart, we spent so much time online together (gaming, IM, Skype, webcam, you name it) that there wasn't much room for surprises for the actual in-person meeting. [*EVE Online*, female, 24]

Falling in love in an online game doesn't mean that the only interactions occur in the game behind game avatars. Getting a sense of how the other person looks and behaves outside the game is very much the expectation even in these online relationships.

Given that people from all over the world play online games, it makes sense that large geographic distances often separate these romantic couples. In many cases, the players lived in different countries. This distance complicates meeting face-to-face for both logistical and financial reasons. Players working or in college would have to plan around their vacation schedules, and these first dates have a significant up-front cost for the plane ticket. These logistical and financial obstacles make the relationship harder rather than easier. Having to pay for a plane ticket to your first date certainly complicates things.

> Once we both realized that a rather large ocean might not be too large of a barrier, he made plans to visit around Christmas. [*EverQuest II*, female, 32]

> I should point out that we were on other sides of the Atlantic, me in London in the UK, and her near Chicago in the US, which made the relationship easier and harder. [*World of Warcraft*, male, 28]

> I was very resistant to [the idea of having a relationship] at first, even though I was attracted to him, because of the age and geographical differences (he was from Canada; I'm from the U.S.). He was persistent, though, and eventually I gave in. [*City of Heroes*, female, 31]

Even though almost all of these players had traded photographs and seen each other on webcams, stepping off the plane to meet their romantic partner face-to-face for the first time was still understandably a nerve-wracking experience.

> A month later he flew to Wisconsin to meet me, and it was a wonderful but almost frighteningly intense experience. From the first day that

we spent together, we both felt very intensely that we belonged together (though neither of us admitted it until several months later), which was very confusing. [*World of Warcraft*, female, 30]

It was a challenge to work out the logistics of the thing, but ultimately, it was worth it. The first meeting? Well, I spent all day on a plane, got to my final destination exhausted and ready for dinner. When I laid eyes on my future wife, I felt the exhaustion melt away and my hunger remained, but I no longer wanted dinner. [*EverQuest*, male, 25]

I spent the flights to her (I had to change planes) in the same nervous and excited state (I was very impatient to get there, the planes seemed to take forever and a day), and I was particularly nervous that fate might intervene and I might be somehow denied entry to the US (I wasn't, of course). . . . Two years after that we're married and living in the UK! :) [*World of Warcraft*, male, 28]

There were many happy endings to the stories. Many of the couples had moved to be together geographically, and some had married or indicated plans for marriage.

That was five years ago and we are still together, happy, and working on the future. From online start to present day, we've been best friends for nine years now. We still game together, too! [*World of Warcraft*, female, 33]

It has been nearly 5 years and we are still together. I moved from the US to Europe a few years ago and there are no regrets. [*EverQuest II*, female, 32]

We are still together, happily married and adopting our first child. [*Martial Heroes*, female, 35]

Of the stories that did not have happy endings, some found the distance to be an insurmountable problem, while others mentioned typical personality-based problems.

It could have been a very good relationship had we lived closer. That was the only real difference, and no, we decided neither of us could move closer together (we each had children). [*EverQuest II*, female, 49]

Our relationship ended after about 6 months in a heartbreaking situation for both. He needed more than I could provide online, and I needed someone more stable and less clingy. [*World of Warcraft*, female, 22]

Of course, meeting someone online is not restricted to meeting while gaming. The rise of online games coincided with the rise of online dating websites. Match.com went into live beta in 1995 and was profiled by *Wired* magazine that year. eHarmony launched in 2000. In that same timeframe, *Ultima Online*, *EverQuest*, *Lineage*, and other games appeared. But meeting someone in an online game is very different from meeting someone in an online dating site. First of all, none of the players in the survey mentioned that they were looking for love in an online game. In fact, they often mentioned the exact opposite.[5]

I was in no way "looking" for anyone. . . . In fact I turned down advances I received in real life citing I was not ready to start dating up again because I had just gotten out of a serious relationship. [*World of Warcraft*, female, 24]

I wasn't looking for this to happen, it just did. [*City of Villains*, female, 25]

Because there were no expectations of love, players getting to know each other were not burdened with the pressures and awkwardness of first dates. More often than not, players had grouped together and chatted with each other a great deal before love became part of the equation. To suggest that online relationships are inherently superficial is to ignore the far more obvious lie that people are exactly themselves on first dates.

> I believe that the online environment made it much easier. There was nothing in the way of awkward social pressure that is the "first date." It started out with two people of the opposite sex talking and having fun with absolutely no expectations of romance or sex. [EverQuest, male, 25]

> We were able to be more honest with each other without worrying about looks or sex and all of the pressure and distractions that go along with that. [World of Warcraft, female, 22]

Falling in love in an online game is more similar to an office romance than finding someone in an online dating site. The love grows out of working with and getting to know another person. It is these opportunities of working together with someone that online games excel at. As many players pointed out, working together with someone through a difficult situation is revealing. Seeing how someone reacts to unfair criticisms, unplanned mishaps, and their own mistakes can reveal a lot. Sitting together in silence in a movie theater tells you much less in comparison.

> We'd tackled life-threatening crises together before we ever went on our first date. [World of Warcraft, female, 32]

> EQ was a great way to see how a potential partner treated others. [World of Warcraft, female, 22]

It bears emphasizing that most of these players got to learn about each other before romantic feelings were sparked. In short, they spent time getting to know each other without the intent of trying to date or get in bed with each other. The typical geographical separation further inhibits romantic intentions because these players often assume that they're talking to someone they will never meet face-to-face.

> I believe you get to learn more about a person's feelings when you meet them online, because it is easier to talk to someone whom you originally think you won't meet IRL, and thus won't be embarrassed to tell them secrets about you. [*Ragnarok Online*, male, 23]

> I think the Internet makes it easier to be more open with people about your likes, dislikes, feelings, etc., because, most of the time, you know you're never going to meet them and so can be freer with information. [*World of Warcraft*, female, 36]

The fact that love is sidelined in online games seems one reason why relationships can work so well. People can get to know each other first without love getting in the way.

Although anonymity can make it easier to lie online, in gaming the lack of romantic pressures and the belief that you're talking to someone you'll never meet can have the opposite effect.

> In my case, because we were talking in chat, almost anonymously in a sense, I think it made it easier for us to get to know each other, because we could say things that might have been hard for slightly "stiff-upper-lip" type people like us to express in real life. [*World of Warcraft*, male, 28]

Many studies have repeatedly shown that people may actually become more open and forthcoming when interacting over a computer. When clinical psychologists began using computers for initial patient interviews, they found that "highly personal, and therefore potentially embarrassing, information is sometimes more easily revealed to a computer." In a study of online newsgroup users, respondents strongly agreed with the statement that they could "confide in this person about almost anything" and strongly disagreed that they "would never tell this person anything intimate or personal about myself." In my own survey of online gamers, I found that 24 percent of players had told personal issues or secrets to their online friends that they had never told their offline friends. In an online chat, when one person shares something intimate about him- or herself, the other person often reciprocates. This feedback loop, paired with the tendency to idealize chat partners online, creates what computer-mediated communication expert Joe Walther has called "hyperpersonal interactions"—interactions that feel much more intimate than typical face-to-face exchanges. Thus, trust and intimacy can evolve more quickly online than face-to-face.[6]

These points underscore an important aspect of the Joan story I described at the start of this chapter. In a forest of liars, no one needs to call out the liar. The reason why Joan's deception caused such an outrage was precisely because all her friends thought they were having honest and intimate conversations with one another. If most people were liars on CompuServe, the community couldn't have existed. By the same token, if most people were liars on CompuServe, there would have been no outrage over Joan. If anything, the shared outrage highlights what is seldom pointed out in Joan's story—that her friends were outraged because they themselves were sharing honest and intimate stories. Although this story is often used as a parable of deception online, I would argue that it is a parable of honesty online. For Joan's story to work and make sense, the unspoken assumption is that the majority of people online are telling the truth.

Of course, nothing prevents people from outright lying online. Whenever gamers in my survey mentioned deception, their sense of vigilance was apparent. Given the pervasive notion that online relationships are impossible, it's easy to understand why many people think that gamers who get involved in an online relationship are naive and impulsive people who are putting themselves at great risk.

But it is actually these very people who readily acknowledge the risk and are typically hypervigilant about it. In many of their stories, players made it clear that honesty was important to them and brought the issue up explicitly in their interactions.

> The main reason that our on-line relationship worked out so well is that we were completely honest with each other from the get-go. Whenever people ask me if I was worried that he wouldn't be who he said he was on-line, I reply, "He told me he was 30, an accountant, and was losing his hair. I was pretty sure he wasn't lying!" [*World of Warcraft*, female, 30]

> As we were really interested in each other and the lives we'd led and so on, and both truthful to the point of painfulness, rather than trying to paint prettier pictures of ourselves, I think we communicated very well. [*World of Warcraft*, male, 28]

> It's harder and can be dangerous if people aren't honest. Both he and I weren't "on the make" and weren't trying to impress anyone or each other, so we were completely ourselves, honest about our likes and dislikes and opinions. [*EverQuest II*, female, 47]

The communication cascade is a part of this vigilance. By trading photos and using webcams, players are making sure that the person is who he or she says they are.

> I didn't really have much of a surprise when I met him for the first time, I'd seen him in photos, through a webcam, and heard him on the phone for around 6 months straight prior to meeting him. [*EverQuest*, female, 34]

This same vigilance has been observed by others. In a study of 202 users of a newsgroup focused on online dating, one major theme that emerged was high levels of caution, even among people who have had successful relationships. For example, one respondent wrote, "While the majority of people online are genuine, you have to protect yourself from those who are not." This pairing of explicit vigilance with personal anxiety was also a prominent feature of the narratives I collected.[7]

> Before I met him, I did worry a lot about if all that he told me was true. When I met him, there were no surprises, he and his family were exactly who they said they were. [FlyFF, female, 21]

Making the Impossible Possible

Now that we've seen how these online relationships typically unfold and some of their unique features, let's finally turn to why 60 percent of the gamers in the survey didn't think their relationships would have worked out had they first met their partner offline. Two specific reasons were mentioned repeatedly.

As I read through their stories, it surprised me how often the gamers, without any prompting from the questions, described either themselves or their partners as being shy.

> My now-husband was very shy, but obviously a very sweet guy. [World of Warcraft, female, 30]

> I find myself to be a very shy and introverted person in real life. . . . Due to my social personality, most women had overlooked me as shy, not confident or any of my other redeeming qualities. [World of Warcraft, male, 25]

About 25 percent of participants mentioned shyness somewhere in their story. And a good handful of them pointed at shyness (in themselves or their partners) as the specific reason why the relationship wouldn't have happened in a face-to-face situation.

> Since we are both shy, we probably would not have talked in real life. . . . Then again, I've always liked the cute shy ones, so who knows. ;) [EverQuest II, female, 20]

He is shy and very reserved and I do think he would let the opportunity pass him by. It is sad to admit that, but it is the truth. [*World of Warcraft*, female, 29]

If I had met her in RL first neither of us would've stepped up to make the first move due to our shyness. [*FlyFF*, male, 38]

We are both shy and introverted people, so if we had met each other in real life first, we probably wouldn't have been brave enough to reveal ourselves as honestly as we did online. [*FlyFF*, female, 21]

Chatting with someone online is very different from chatting with someone face-to-face. Of course, it's very easy to point out all the things that are missing. You can't see the other person's facial expressions. You're missing out on the tone of his or her voice. All you have is the text. But less isn't necessarily worse. Studies have shown that people who are shy are more likely to develop close friendships and fall in love online. And the player narratives here push this one step further. The online environment didn't only make it easier for these players to get to know someone. The online game allowed players to develop a genuine relationship with someone whom they felt would have been impossible to date in the physical world. Even if these players met face-to-face in the physical world, the relationship probably wouldn't have happened. In the case of these players, less is actually more.[8]

Players often mentioned another reason why these relationships wouldn't have happened face-to-face. When we see the elves and gnomes in an online game, it's easy to portray online relationships as deceptive. How can you have a relationship with something that doesn't exist in the real world? But we forget that people are superficial in the physical world, too, just in different ways. In fact, this was the very reason why many of the gamers didn't think that the relationship would have started had they met first face-to-face. They would have immediately written the other person off because of a physical trait. The other person was too young, too tall, too thin, too blue-collar, or simply not their physical "type."

> I probably would not have developed this relationship in RL. She isn't my typical love interest but because I got to know her emotionally first, I was able to find someone that was a perfect fit. [EverQuest II, male, 32]

> Ironically, we would not have had a relationship if we had first met at a party or something. Neither of us was the other's "type," and our age difference would have been obvious and a barrier to both of us. [World of Warcraft, female, 59]

> I would never have dated this person in real life. Totally different worlds. I am a grad student and he works in the service industry. Our paths would not have crossed. We lived in different countries. This is the relationship :) On the outside we seem totally opposite. But we work so well on the inside. I guess that is what comes of meeting inside out :p . [World of Warcraft, female, 25]

> I doubt we would have had a relationship if we had met in real life. At first glance, I'd say he definitely wasn't my type. Too nice, too accommodating, without a sense of adventure. I would have pigeonholed him without ever giving him a chance. [World of Warcraft, female, 25]

Again, most people can easily think of the ways in which online communication is "less" than talking face-to-face, but as we've seen over and over again, less can be more. When you can't see what someone looks like, you can't judge him or her simply based on looks. By taking looks out of the equation, these players were forced to actually learn about the other person instead of making a snap judgment. The online game forced players to focus on who a person is rather than what he or she looks like.

The *World of Warcraft* player's phrase "inside out" is particularly apt. In face-to-face relationships, we first see how people look and dress, and we learn their names. And then slowly over time, we learn about their passions, fears, and personal hang-ups. In an online game, it tends to work the other way around. How a person treats others or reacts in a crisis piques our interest. Then, after getting to know that person, we may learn about where he or she lives, does for a living, and is called. And only after many interactions do we trade photos and finally get to learn what the other person looks like.

> With gaming together, you can screen people's quirks, their political views, temperament, religious beliefs, without the clouding of RL sex and lust complicating it. You can become friends FIRST. Then when you meet in real life AFTER developing the relationship, it's just, wow. [*EverQuest II*, female, 47]

> The game WAS the reason we fell in love. Going through all the adventures and quests together really built our relationship. We found out how the other person is when they are mad, tired, sad, happy, excited, annoyed (etc.). We got to know each other without the physical aspect of the relationship and I believe that made our emotional connection sooooo much stronger. [*City of Villains*, female, 25]

Relationships online certainly develop differently than relationships offline, but different doesn't automatically mean worse. Virtual worlds can negate some of the superficial aspects of face-to-face relationships.

A Modern-Day Fairy Tale

On a sunny Sunday in 1998, Clark Rockefeller carried his seven-year-old daughter on his shoulders down the streets of Boston. He was forty-seven, claiming descent from the Percy Rockefeller branch of the clan, and recently divorced from his ex-wife, a senior partner at the global management-consulting firm McKinsey and Company. His wife won custody of their daughter, and this was one of the three restricted visits each year he was permitted with his daughter. To add insult to injury, these visits were under the supervision of a social worker.

As they approached his limousine, Clark pushed the social worker away and sped away with his daughter. This kidnapping would unravel the secrets of Clark's life. "Clark Rockefeller" was one of three aliases the man had created over thirty years. Before he was Clark Rockefeller, he was Clark Crowe, a movie producer living in Connecticut. Before that, he was Christopher Chichester, a descendant of British royalty living in San Marino. This man, actually a German immigrant named Christopher Gerharts Reiter, arrived in the United States in 1978. Even though he didn't finish college and had limited savings, he managed to climb the social ladder through deception. He was hired as the head of the US offices of Nikko Securities on Wall Street in 1987 even though he had absolutely no experience in securities. He became a member of many private gentleman's clubs on Wall Street. And he married a woman who had an MBA from Harvard. To say he fooled a lot of people would be an understatement.[9]

You don't need virtual worlds to weave elaborate personas. Our obsession with pointing out dishonesty online ignores the deception and superficiality that occur offline. And one first fundamental truth of virtual worlds is simply that the people you meet online live in the physical world.

In fairy tales like "Snow White" or "Cinderella," the all-good fairy godmothers and the all-evil stepmothers aren't merely one-dimensional caricatures of human intentions. This storytelling device serves a powerful function for children. Child psychologist Bruno

Bettelheim argues that these characters create a coping mechanism for children to deal with their own mothers when they get angry or become scary. Because children have a hard time making sense of how someone so loving can suddenly become so scary, this splitting mechanism allows them to keep the kind-mother separate from the scary-mother.[10]

We have been telling ourselves a modern-day fairy tale about truth and falsehood simplistically partitioned into two worlds. Too often, media stories about the Internet revolve around the myth that truth and honesty reside in the physical world while fantasy and deception reside in the online world. This is the unspoken logic underlying the sensationalist stories of people finding love online—the drama comes from the tacit question of how people can find true love in a world of falsehoods. By splitting realities, we ignore the fact that honesty and deception are very much a part of both the physical and virtual worlds. As we've seen, people can be quite superficial in the real world. We often assume that fantasy avatars hide the truth, but fantasy avatars can actually reveal the truth. For some people, fantasy worlds allow them to form genuine relationships that couldn't have started in the physical world.

These findings about how people fall in love in online games also reveal an important aspect about relationships in general. Online dating websites often tout their scientific matchmaking methods, many of which rely on long surveys of personality traits and attitudes. The underlying premise is that a lasting relationship can be predicted with an extensive checklist of either similar or complementary traits. This claim taps into a fairy-tale fantasy: there is a perfect prince or princess out there waiting for you if you search hard enough. Unfortunately, there is no empirical evidence to back up these matchmaking methods. A recent review of the psychological literature has shown that similarities between a couple's personalities account for roughly 0.5 percent of their relationship satisfaction. There is even less evidence that complementarity leads to happy relationships. It turns out that relationships are more than just checklists. Rather than being tools for sophisticated matchmaking, online dating sites may work simply because they provide a roster of single people in your area who are receptive to dating.

The player narratives in this chapter provide a very different perspective of how relationships work. Players developed relationships after going through adventures together and sharing in both disappointments and accomplishments. Relationships are created when two people are willing to work through life's ups and downs together, whether online or offline and regardless of what their checklists look like. Lasting relationships are forged, not found. And the truth is that relationships are a lot of work. This is why online dating websites are so seductive. They are selling the myth that compatible relationships can be deduced with a magical database and require no real work on your part. For both good and bad, online games turn out to be a lot of work. And lasting relationships happen in online games because the gameplay often forces people to build trust and work together. These games jumpstart that forging process.[11]

CHAPTER 8 TOOLS OF PERSUASION AND CONTROL

In the last five chapters, I've described how offline categories—such as our ethnicity or gender—find a way to contaminate the assumed utopias of virtual worlds. But the Proteus Paradox isn't just about how our offline politics don't change when we enter virtual worlds, it's also about how things beyond our control end up altering how we think and behave. In this and the remaining chapters, I'll detail how virtual worlds provide unparalleled tools for controlling us.

We're all liars. We're trained to lie to each other in very specific ways so that we immediately forgive each other. And the aisles of supermarkets and drugstores supply us with a vast arsenal of these tools of deception. There are toothpastes and peroxide strips to make your teeth whiter. There are hair-coloring products to cover your grays, and lotions and powders to smooth your complexion. And there are pushup bras and compression shirts to enhance your appearance. As a society, we not only tolerate these modest and temporary self-transformations, we encourage them. No one will get mad at you because your teeth are a little whiter. By conforming to these ideals of appearance, we create a favorable impression on people we meet and interact with. We call it "dressing to impress" or "putting your best face forward." But what does it mean to put your best face forward in a virtual world in which you can swap faces at the click of a mouse button? Virtual worlds like *Second Life* feature an extreme form of customization; as the company's product factsheet states, "Using over 150 unique sliders, change everything from your foot size to your eye color to the cut of your shirt." What are the consequences of being in a world in which facial reconstructive surgery is neither expensive nor painful but cheap and instantaneous?[1]

Stealing Faces

When you play a video game on a screen with a resolution of 1900 × 1200 pixels, your eyes receive over 2 million pixels every second. Amazingly, not only do our brains process that information continuously, but gamers can react and respond with lightning reflexes. To accomplish this feat, our brains highlight and prioritize the processing of patterns or points of interest. Faces are a good example of these privileged patterns. Even babies, ten minutes after being born, pay more attention to images that resemble a face than scrambled versions of those same images. Their brains quickly pick out any visual patterns that resemble an oval with two eyes, a nose, and a mouth placed appropriately.[2]

Our brains employ many other heuristics to sort through the information deluge of everyday life almost instantaneously. After we pick out faces in this visual data stream, we next need to decide how to react to those faces, the bodies they are attached to, and the gestures their hands are producing. When we meet a stranger at a social gathering, we don't pause the conversation for a minute to sort through this information consciously and then weigh the pros and cons of whether this is someone we want to meet. Instead, a gut feeling drives our interactions with this stranger. One cue that our brains use to make these snap judgments is how similar the other person is to us. We perceive people who look like us or believe in the same things we do as more attractive and more persuasive than people with whom we share little.[3]

Our brains don't have much time to make these decisions, so it turns out that even entirely arbitrary points of similarity can make us like another person more. In a study conducted by psychologist Jerry Burger and his colleagues, undergraduate students met another student taking part in the study—actually a research assistant posing as a participant (a "confederate" in experimental design jargon). During the study, half of the students discovered that they "coincidentally" shared the same birthday with the confederate. The other half, the control group, did not share the same birthday. After the study ostensibly ended, the confederate asked each student if, as part of a class assignment, he or she would mind reading an eight-page essay and providing a one-page critique in just twenty-four hours. The students who thought that they shared the same birthday with the confederate were almost twice as likely to agree to this burdensome request than were those in the control group. Using the same study framework, Burger and his colleagues found that the same effect could be elicited if the students were led to believe that they shared the same first name or fingerprint patterns with the confederate.[4]

If faces are given priority treatment by our brains, and similarity leads to attraction and cooperation, could we leverage the extreme customization of virtual worlds, not to create new faces, but to create strangers that look like you? Instead of stealing your birthday or your first name, these virtual strangers could literally steal your face. Of course, this transformation is impossible in the physical world. You could dye your hair or wear colored contacts, but there is no easy way to change your facial bone structure to match another person's face. In the digital world, however, this is an easy problem to solve. Commercially available software allows you to blend two digital photographs by indicating points of reference—the corners of the eye, the hairline, and so on. This makes it possible to create a virtual stranger whose face shares a precise 20 percent or 40 percent resemblance to your face.

On the eve of the 2004 presidential election between George W. Bush and John Kerry, my graduate adviser, Jeremy Bailenson, was chatting with another professor in the communication department with a background in political science, Shanto Iyengar, about face morphing technology. Because people are more attracted to and more likely to help someone who looks like them, they wondered if they could influence how people voted in an election by blending people's faces into well-known political candidates. In short, if a political candidate looked a little more like you, would you be more likely to vote for him or her? Another graduate student, Nathan Collins, and I were brought onboard the project. Even though past studies suggested that similarity cues increased attraction and persuasion, it wasn't at all clear that it would matter in a high-stakes situation like a presidential election in which people had strong feelings about the candidates. And given how often people had seen posters and television ads of both candidates, it also wasn't clear whether we could tamper with their faces at all without people noticing immediately.

We decided to hedge our bets. We would use a conservative 20 percent face morph for half the study sample and a higher-risk 40 percent morph for the other half. The 160 study participants were a nationally representative sample of voting-age US citizens recruited by Knowledge Networks, a company that offers free web TV in exchange for regular participation in online surveys. The participants were first asked to provide a digital photograph of themselves to allow us to create the morphed candidate images. Then, one week before the presidential election and ostensibly as an entirely separate study, the same participants were shown a photograph of Bush and a photograph of Kerry and asked about their opinions of the candidates and for whom they were likely to vote. Each participant saw one candidate morphed with their face and the other candidate morphed with someone else (to control for any extraneous effects of digital morphing). We found that face morphing made no difference to strong partisans, but weak partisans and independents were swayed by it. Overall, the effect was significant: among the group of participants morphed with Kerry, Kerry received enough votes to win the presidential election.[5]

This study was one of four studies we conducted using face morphing. Altogether, more than six hundred participants were shown digitally morphed photographs blending their faces into political candidates, ranging from 20 percent to 40 percent morphs. In each study, every participant was asked to guess the goal of the experiment. Roughly 3 percent of participants believed that someone had manipulated the candidate's image. Not one participant across the four studies suggested the possibility that his or her own photograph had been blended with the political candidate's. In virtual worlds, tools of persuasion can be powerful yet undetectable.[6]

Breaking Reality

This strange new world of face stealing was where I found myself in 2004, a year into my graduate program at Stanford. For four years, I worked with Jeremy Bailenson in the Virtual Human Interaction Lab on dozens of studies exploring one question: What if you could break reality? This question is rooted in a peculiar feature of virtual worlds. Virtual worlds do such a good job of creating the illusion of shared reality that you have to take a step back to remember that a computer system mediates all the interactions between users. Everything that two people say to each other has to first pass through this digital intermediary. In a world in which two people never have direct contact with each other, the messenger is king. And if you are in control of the virtual world, the messenger is working for you, and thus you become the king.

The implications are far-reaching. In the most simplistic scenario, imagine that the system performs basic sentence parsing and makes sure that all requests contain either the word *please* or a smiley face. If it doesn't, the system simply injects one or the other. Player A is unaware of the injection, and Player B responds more positively than he or she might have, starting off a positive feedback loop. Or these superpowers could be the king's privilege. The king could have a dozen automated helpers injecting mundane pleasantries as needed. The king is always smiling, always saying, "Thank you," and always remembers the names of your spouse, children, and favorite sports team.

But the king's powers go well beyond that. Consider eye gaze. We know that students feel more engaged and learn better if the teacher pays them more attention. In a virtual classroom, each student sees the shared reality of the virtual world only via his or her own individual display device. This means that these many slices of shared reality do not need to line up with each other. Thus, the teacher in a virtual classroom can maintain eye contact with every single student at the same time. Each student would feel that he or she has the undivided attention of the teacher. In fact, in a virtual classroom, you can warp space itself. In a physical classroom, only one student can sit in the front center of the classroom. In a virtual classroom, there is no reason why every student cannot sit in the front center of the classroom, each perceiving the other students dynamically repositioned around him or her.

We also know that an unruly student can distract other students in a classroom. In a virtual classroom, the king can automatically censor the unruly behavior, splicing in a loop of recorded good behavior from a moment ago and projecting that instead to the other students. By placing students in a roomful of perfectly attentive students, we increase the likelihood that each student conforms to that model behavior. These superpowers could be combined to create the perfect virtual classroom. Indeed, my colleagues and I at Stanford have created these very virtual classrooms, placed students in them, and found that they improved learning.[7]

This broken reality also reveals the true power of face stealing. In a virtual world, a presenter's avatar could be individually blended with each audience member. Audience members each see their own version of reality in which the presenter looks subtly like them. In virtual worlds, political candidates can literally have a thousand faces. And of course, face morphing is only one of many possibly transformations. A benevolent king could create the perfect classroom, but a more devious king might create persuasion chambers tailored to each audience member. The devious king would steal part of your face and maintain eye contact with you while you sit front and center. And of course, the king's teeth will also be that impossible shade of brilliant white.

The Proteus Effect

In 1966, psychologist Stuart Valins conducted a lab experiment in which male undergraduate students were asked to look at models from a *Playboy* magazine while they were hooked up to a machine that amplified their heartbeat and made it audible. The students were told that the experiment was a study of physiological reactions to visual stimuli. Of course, because this was a psychological experiment, the machine wasn't actually amplifying their heartbeat. It wasn't recording anything at all. Instead, the heartbeat noises had been prerecorded and were being played back by the machine. When the students were looking at some of the models, they would hear their "heartbeat" increase noticeably. At the end of the study, the students were asked to rate the attractiveness of each model. The students rated models randomly paired with an increased heartbeat as being more attractive.

But why should a bogus heartbeat influence how students rated the models? Wouldn't the students have formed an impression of each model based solely on the photograph? Deciphering our own emotions and attitudes is not straightforward; we do not keep an up-to-date reference list of our attitudes toward every person, situation, or social issue we might encounter. In many cases, our own thoughts are a black box, even to ourselves. We do this self-deciphering without conscious thought because this is how we understand other people. We don't have direct access to other people's inner thoughts and must infer their attitudes based on how they behave. Whenever Sam comes home, the first thing he does is sit down in front of the TV and play video games. He probably likes video games. Whenever the art lesson starts, Rachel slumps in her chair and frowns. She probably doesn't like art lessons. In the same way that we use other people's behavior to infer their attitudes, we do the same with our own black box. We unconsciously and automatically observe our own behaviors to make sense of how we feel about something. Thus, in Valins's study, the students notice their rapid heartbeat, and since the only stimulus in the room is the *Playboy* model, it must be the cause of their arousal. And if they are aroused, the model must be very attractive. This self-perception theory reverses our intuitive understanding of how our brains work. Our behavior isn't directed by our attitudes. It's the other way around. Our behaviors direct our attitudes.[8]

Of course, real life is never as sterile as a psychology lab. The cause of our excitement or sadness at any given moment can be ambiguous and difficult to pinpoint, especially in the typical data deluge our brains receive. This leads to many interesting accidents. The Capilano Suspension Bridge is a 5-foot-wide, 450-foot-long pedestrian bridge that stretches over the Capilano River in North Vancouver, British Columbia, with a 230-foot drop to the rocks and rapids below. The low handrails and the bridge's tendency to tilt and wobble as one crosses it create the constant impression that one is about to fall. In 1974, psychologists Donald Dutton and Arthur Aron conducted a study on the bridge specifically because of its "arousal-inducing features." A solid wood bridge conveniently located upriver served as the control condition. On each of the two bridges, a female research assistant approached male tourists as they approached the midpoint of the bridge and asked them to fill out a questionnaire for her psychology class. When the tourists finished the questionnaire, the research assistant gave them her phone number and told them to call her later if they wanted to know more about the study. Tourists who met the female assistant on the suspension bridge were more likely to call her afterward than were the tourists who met her on the solid bridge. In Valins's bogus heartbeat study, the students attributed their arousal to the photograph. In the bridge study, the arousal caused by crossing a shaky bridge was incorrectly attributed to presence of the female assistant. This caused the men to be more attracted to the female assistant and thus more likely to call her later.[9]

We decipher our own attitudes based not only on what we do but also on what we wear. In the mid-1980s, psychologists Mark Frank and Thomas Gilovich tabulated past records from the National Football League and the National Hockey League. They discovered that teams wearing black uniforms received more penalties than teams wearing uniforms of other colors. Because teams change uniform color depending on where they play, Frank and Gilovich were able to show that when the same team wore black uniforms, it received more penalties. They also found that people perceive players in black uniforms as being more aggressive on the field. This led them to wonder if wearing a black uniform made players more aggressive via self-perception. To exclude the possibility of referee bias, they conducted a lab experiment. They brought students into the lab in groups of three, randomly assigned each group either black or white uniforms, and led the students to believe that they would be competing against another team of students preparing in another room. Each group then saw a list of twelve games from which to choose the five they wished to compete against the other team in. Frank and Gilovich found that study participants given black uniforms selected more aggressive games than participants given white uniforms. In their words, "Just as observers see those in black uniforms as tough, mean, and aggressive, so too does the person wearing that uniform."[10]

By 2005, I had worked with Bailenson for two years, exploring how transformations in virtual worlds could grant social superpowers—how a digital transformation could influence people's interactions. I began to wonder if there was anything to the flipside of that question. Your avatar in a virtual world or online game is like a super uniform. It is infinitely more fluid and encompassing than a black outfit. Your age, your gender, and your body proportions are all things that are easily modified in a virtual world. And if a simple black uniform can make someone more aggressive in a laboratory, what happens to you when you are put into a digital avatar?

Many aspects of everyday human psychology are well studied and known. Unfortunately, some of the findings are truly depressing. One example is the unfair advantage that attractiveness bestows. The well-known maxims "Beauty is in the eye of the beholder" and "Beauty is skin deep," though comforting, are both empirically false. In a meta-analysis of eighteen hundred studies on attractiveness, Judith Langlois and her colleagues found that both within and across cultures, people agree on who is and is not attractive. In addition, attractive people are perceived to be more capable in their jobs, more competent in social situations, better adjusted, and more fun to talk to. They are also paid more attention, given better rewards, and in general treated more favorably in social interactions. As has been long documented, these lifelong positive biases have tangible benefits. Attractive people do better in their careers, have dated more people, have had sex with more people, are more confident, more extraverted, and in better physical and mental health than people who are less attractive. As one concrete example out of many similar papers, one study found that attractive criminal defendants received lighter sentences than less attractive defendants.[11]

If giving football and hockey players black uniforms makes them more aggressive, Bailenson and I wondered whether giving people attractive avatars would make them more extraverted. Could a lifelong disposition be altered by something as intangible and transient as a series of pixels on a screen? At the Stanford lab, we had a secret weapon that improved our odds. Instead of a typical desktop virtual world, we had an immersive virtual reality lab. Users donned a head-mounted display with a small, high-resolution screen for each eye (thus allowing stereoscopic vision). The headgear had a small infrared light that was tracked continuously by four cameras, one at each corner of the room. An embedded accelerometer, like the ones found in iPhones and Nintendo Wii remotes, tracked the user's rotation. Thus, when the user moved forward, the cameras would track the infrared light and update the virtual world accordingly. When the user turned, the accelerometer would track the rotation, and the user's perspective in the virtual world would change. The system had a refresh rate of 60 Hz, permitting a seamless, immersive experience with no detectable lag. More important, no keyboarding or mousing was needed to navigate this virtual environment. To walk forward in the virtual world, you simply walked forward in the physical world. To look up in the virtual world, you looked up in the physical world. Thus, someone could come to our lab, put on the goggles, and immediately find himself or herself walking around in a European city, a high school classroom, or a rainforest jungle.

It's hard to explain how fast people forget about their physical surroundings when they put the goggles on. One popular demo we had was a virtual ten-foot-deep pit in the middle of a virtual room with a wooden plank running across the top. Some people chose not to cross the plank when given the option. Those who did walk the plank were often visibly nervous and jittery. Whenever we ran this demo, we had to assign a research assistant to catch the person should he or she start to fall—people's bodies reacted to the virtual falling automatically, and they would begin to crouch and lose their balance. I was soon relieved of this duty when Bailenson noticed that I was horrible at catching people before they fell down.

For our study, we created a virtual world that was an exact replica of the physical lab room. This may seem strange, but it solved a practical problem. Without clearly marked boundaries in the virtual world, people would crash into the physical walls of the lab and hurt themselves. The easiest, albeit uncreative, way to prevent this was to replicate the walls in the virtual environment. In the study itself, we randomly assigned students to either an attractive or an unattractive avatar. Because the immersive virtual environment provided a first-person perspective, we created a virtual mirror for participants to see their virtual selves. On the other side of the virtual room was a stranger, controlled by a research assistant. This virtual stranger would greet the participant and ask the participant to come closer. The stranger would then ask the participant to introduce him- or herself using the prompt, "Tell me a little about yourself." We found that people given attractive avatars walked almost three feet closer to the stranger than people given unattractive avatars. They also shared more pieces of personal information with the stranger. These findings were consistent with the self-perception effect. People conformed to the expectations of their avatar's appearance. The brief exposure to an attractive avatar made participants more gregarious with a virtual stranger.[12]

We implemented several safeguards to rule out alternative explanations. For example, we know that people treat attractive people more positively. This means that the effect of the attractive avatar could actually be driven by the confederate's reactions, not the self-perception effect. To prevent this, we programmed the virtual world such that the confederate always saw the participant's avatar with the same stock face. In other words, only the study participant saw his or her "real" face. Another potential explanation is that the attractiveness or unattractiveness of the faces was so blatant that participants were consciously role-playing social stereotypes or unconsciously yielding to the expectations of the researchers. To test for this, we asked participants to guess the goals of the study. Almost all thought that we were comparing an immersive virtual interaction with a face-to-face or desktop virtual world interaction. No participant mentioned attractiveness or thought that attractiveness was being manipulated in the study.

Even though Bailenson and I had found that a subtle manipulation in avatar attractiveness led to noticeable differences in how people behave in virtual worlds, we wondered whether this was an idiosyncratic outcome, perhaps unique to attractiveness or the specific virtual interaction. So we picked another variable to test. Like the unfair advantage of attractiveness, height is a well-studied and depressing psychological variable. We perceive taller people to be more competent, more confident, and better suited to be leaders. In fact, height translates into tangible differences in income. In 2004, business school professors Timothy Judge and Daniel Cable gathered data from more than eight thousand people from four sources of labor statistics and found that each inch of increase in height leads to a projected increase in annual earnings of roughly $800. A person who is six feet tall earns $5,525 more each year than someone who is five feet, five inches, even after controlling for gender, weight, and age.[13]

At the lab, we wondered if giving someone a taller avatar would make them more confident. We again put participants into a virtual environment modeled on the physical lab and had them interact with a stranger. But instead of using an introductory prompt, we had participants in the study play a bargaining game with the confederate. We asked the participant and the confederate to share a hypothetical pool of $100. One would offer a split, and the other would either accept or reject the split. If the both parties accepted the split, they would share the money accordingly. If one rejected the split, neither would receive any money. There were four rounds of this game. The participant would make the split in the first round, and we scripted the confederate to accept this split every time. In the second round, the confederate would make an even 50–50 split. In the third round, the participant would make the split again. But in the final round, the confederate would make an unfair split of 75–25 in his or her own favor. This negotiation exercise would reveal two things: How aggressively does the participant bargain? And what does he or she do when an unfair offer is made?

The participants in the study were given avatars that were either the same height, ten centimeters (four inches) taller, or ten centimeters shorter than the confederate's avatar. All participants offered near-even splits in the first round, so there was no difference between the height conditions. But during the third round, people given taller avatars made an offer (in their own favor) that was on average almost $10 more than people given shorter avatars. And when the confederate made the unfair offer in the final round, people given taller avatars were half as likely to accept it as people given shorter avatars. As with the attractiveness study, we programmed the virtual world such that the confederate was blind to the participant's virtual height (with the help of a little trigonometry). And when asked to guess the goals of the study, again no participant mentioned that avatar height had been manipulated.[14]

Together, these two studies show that subtle manipulations in avatar appearance have dramatic effects on how people interact with each other in virtual worlds. And these effects occur rapidly, fewer than sixty seconds after being in a new digital body. We think of avatars as things of our own creation, digital clay that can be endlessly shaped. But avatar creation is actually a two-way process. The fact is that our avatars change us in turn. As discussed in the Introduction, Bailenson and I labeled this phenomenon the Proteus Effect after the Greek sea god who was capable of assuming many forms.

These two studies also led us to think about online gamers who spend on average twenty hours each week in virtual worlds. The lab studies showed how avatars change behavior within the virtual world, but what happens when people step back into the physical world? Does the Proteus Effect immediately disappear once the user logs out, or does it transfer to subsequent interactions outside the virtual world? We decided to rerun the attractiveness study with a twist. After coming out of the immersive virtual environment, the students participated in a separate study on online dating among college students. This study took place in front of a standard desktop computer, and the students created profiles on a mock online dating website geared toward college students. After creating their profile and answering some basic personality questions, they saw a grid of nine photographs of college students (from a different university) and selected the two people from the grid they were most interested in meeting. We found that study participants who embodied an attractive avatar in the virtual environment subsequently selected more attractive people from the grid to meet. Even when the students were no longer in a virtual world and interacting using a different technology altogether, their avatar's appearance still mattered.[15]

Digital Doppelgängers

In 2008, the McKinsey Global Institute estimated that two-thirds of baby boomers born between 1945 and 1955 have not saved enough money to maintain their lifestyle in retirement. The 2012 Retirement Confidence Survey revealed that more than half of current workers have not tried to calculate how much money they will need to save for retirement. It is not easy to defer immediate gratification for an incredibly intangible future thirty or forty years down the road. The desires and payoffs of the present moment are always concrete and known—a bigger TV, Starbucks lattes every morning, a fancier car. The desires of your future, retired self are a vague abstraction at best, especially for young college grads starting their first job. This is what makes it so difficult to save money for retirement. It requires the discipline to defer an immediate, known, concrete reward for an undefined and unknown benefit decades in the future.[16]

Hal Hershfield, a professor at the New York University Stern School of Business, used avatars to bring the future forward. Instead of putting participants in a different person's body, Hershfield put undergraduate students in avatars modeled from photographs of their faces. In half of these self avatars, Hershfield left the faces unaltered. In the other half, he digitally aged the faces to realistically add white hair, wrinkles, and sagging skin. As in the attractiveness study, the students saw themselves in a virtual mirror. The students then had to imagine that they had just received a windfall of $1,000. Their task was to allocate that sum among four options: buying a gift for someone special, investing in a retirement fund, planning an extravagant occasion, and putting the money into a checking account. The students who were given avatars of their seventy-year-old selves put twice the amount of money into their retirement accounts compared with students in avatars of their current selves. By bringing the future forward, Hershfield took an intangible, older self and made it visible and salient to college students.[17]

Instead of using virtual worlds to put people in fantasy bodies, Hershfield's study highlighted the power of using virtual worlds to hijack someone's body and face. This painless virtual plastic surgery allows us to change how we think about ourselves and our future. Jesse Fox, a professor of communication at the Ohio State University, took this idea in a different direction. Virtual worlds allow us to change not only how an avatar looks but also how an avatar behaves. In a virtual world, we can replicate your body and then digitally animate it to do anything we want, including things we've never done in the physical world. But why would we want to make digital doppelgängers?

One important way humans learn is by watching other people. Not only do we learn new behaviors by watching others, but we also learn the expected outcomes of a behavior. After all, it would significantly diminish our species' survival if we each individually had to poke our fingers into an electric socket to learn that it is a bad idea. Thus, when we see Peter get praised for playing the piano well, we learn that playing the piano is one way of being rewarded. This in turn makes it more likely we'll go learn to play the piano. But watching someone else is not sufficient. It's important that we are able to identify with this other person. The more similar the person is to us, the more certain it is that our outcomes will match. Thus, if Peter turns out to be a young piano prodigy who has been composing symphonies since he was twelve, most of us probably wouldn't be rushing to learn the piano. But if Peter is roughly our own age, with a similar social background, and is playing quite well after learning the piano for only one month, we may be intrigued enough to take piano lessons. Of course, it is difficult to create the perfect model for a specific person. At best, we may provide an inspiring figure that is of the same gender and roughly the same age.

In contrast, in a virtual world, we can create the perfect model of any person by creating an avatar of him or her. In Fox's study, she brought students into the immersive virtual environment and they watched their digital doppelgängers either run on a treadmill or stand idly in the virtual lab room. In other words, Fox created a digital version of the students that they had no control over. She found that students who had watched their doppelgängers run on the treadmill were more likely to exercise over the next twenty-four hours. Your digital doppelgänger in a virtual world can change how you behave in the real world.[18]

Hijacking the Brain

In the chapter on superstitions, we saw that people are polite to computers because our brains do not differentiate between digital media and human companions. We treat computers as people because technology outpaces human evolution. And superstitions are triggered among online gamers the same way that superstitions are triggered in Skinner's pigeons. This is the same logic that underlies all the studies in virtual environments presented in this chapter. Our brains are harried, overworked processors, besieged by constant information deluges. The automated rules that our brains use to cope with making decisions in everyday life don't care about the media we're using. Our brains make sense of virtual people using the same rules they use for making sense of physical people. When a person looks similar to us, whether we're face-to-face or in a virtual world, we automatically like him or her more.

The difference, of course, is that virtual worlds are infinitely malleable in a way that the physical world is not. There's very little I can do to make myself look more like someone else in the real world, but in the virtual world, this is trivial. Would you like that order of face stealing at 20 percent or 30 percent? This malleability is what allows our cognitive heuristics to be mercilessly hijacked in virtual worlds. Whether it is a manipulation in face stealing or avatar appearance, these undetected changes cause dramatic shifts in behavior both inside and outside of the virtual world. Even the object of our own creation in virtual worlds, our own avatars, can become a tool for behavioral modification. These fantasy worlds of escape can ironically make us susceptible to powerful psychological tools that silently modify our behaviors and attitudes.

In this chapter, I've documented a variety of tools in virtual worlds that can modify our thoughts and behavior, but that doesn't mean these tools can operate only in virtual environments. Of course, these manipulations are easier to deploy in virtual worlds, but a bank or an investment company could generate a customized postcard advertisement with a digitally aged photograph of you if they had access to a reasonably clear photo of you. And these days, especially with the use of social networking sites and Google, it's quite straightforward to find an image of someone. This means that face morphing and doppelgänger techniques could be used in print ads sent to you in the mail or on a banner ad that appears when you're browsing on a website. As Bailenson and I conducted these studies and identified different techniques, we wondered whether people could learn to guard themselves against these persuasion methods—a sort of psychological inoculation. I'm pessimistic for two reasons. First, in many of our studies, participants were not able to detect the subtle manipulations. It is difficult to guard against something that isn't easily detected. And second, most people do not recognize or guard against the plethora of psychological tricks already in use in contemporary advertisements. In the chapter on gender stereotypes, I mentioned the concept of guilt-soothing indulgence in some products targeted at women. Perhaps the best example is the very successful marketing ploy that transformed a cheap and common gemstone into a costly engagement artifact: the diamond ring. The more others know about you, the more tailored and targeted their manipulations can be. They could generate a doppelgänger that not only looked like you but also exhibited similar personality traits. In fact, virtual worlds can be used to infer someone's personality. In the next chapter, I describe how this can be done.

CHAPTER 9   INTROVERTED ELVES, CONSCIENTIOUS GNOMES, AND THE QUEST FOR BIG DATA

Whether it's guilds or raids, online gamers constantly face sudden and stressful decisions. And the decisions they make would seem to be very character revealing. Gaining access to such in-game information, however, is another story. When *World of Warcraft* launched in 2004, Blizzard, the game's developer, allowed players and third-party developers to modify interface elements via a scripting language. Of course, players could not make their characters indestructible or create a sword that killed anything it touched, but these add-ons modified the game interface in interesting and important ways. Some modifications added new buttons and charts on players' screens; others worked silently in the background. There were healing helpers that automatically targeted and cured players who had been poisoned. There were combat add-ons that tracked the average damage output of each team member. There were quest helpers that plotted the most efficient route to complete your current quests. And there were auction helpers that identified and snagged good deals for you in the auction house. None of these add-ons changed the rules or mechanisms of game play, but they provided visibility into the large number of variables being tracked by the game. In order to work, these add-ons had to access Blizzard's server-side data. And this is how the balance of data accessibility began to shift: for the first time, a game company allowed public access to server-side game variables.

What data researchers could access, however, was severely limited. For example, combat helpers could track data only from players in their group. Add-ons could access data only if the character was logged into the game. And add-ons could never access data outside the server the character belonged to. So in theory, everyone's combat data were accessible, but in practice, an add-on had access to only a tiny slice of those data.

In 2005, three research scientists at the Palo Alto Research Center—Nicolas Ducheneaut, Bob Moore, and Eric Nickell—had created a research group studying social interaction and communities in online games called PlayOn. They had created a census add-on tool for *World of Warcraft*. The tool used the "/who" command in the game to return a list of characters who fit certain search parameters. This in-game command let players search for active characters on their server by using a name, name fragment, character class, or character level. Among other things, the command allowed players to search for potential teammates nearby. Instead of searching for a specific character, the PARC census tool returned a list of all active characters on the server. The parameters you could use in searches were also data that the command returned. Thus, the census tool gathered seven variables from every character currently logged on: name, level, class, race, geographical zone, name of guild (if any), and whether the character was currently grouped with other players. The PARC team gathered data from five separate servers at fifteen-minute intervals, twenty-four hours a day, seven days a week. Altogether, the census tool recorded data related to over two hundred thousand unique characters.

In the spring of 2005, after the PARC PlayOn group had accumulated about three months of data, they began looking for a summer intern to help with data analysis. It was a perfect fit for me. I had been playing *World of Warcraft* since its launch, had a few years' experience analyzing large data sets from online gamers, and lived eight minutes away. At the time, we four felt that the data set would make a perfect summer internship project. Even though the data set gathered was vast, there were only seven variables. Our collective intuition that summer was that the interesting findings from the data set would be exhausted in less than three months (the length of my internship), giving us time to write and submit a paper to a conference.

Two years and four papers later, we at last ran out of interesting findings. After the summer internship, I worked part-time at PARC as a research assistant for another two years. We hadn't originally realized that a valuable eighth variable, time, was also being tracked in our growing data warehouse. Not only did we have snapshot data of the seven variables returned by the "/who" command, but because we tracked the servers continuously, we could reconstruct longitudinal profiles of individual gamers—calculating, for example, the speed at which they leveled up. With this metric in hand, we could examine whether a preference for grouping or being in a guild affected a character's rate of advancement.

In addition, the variable of time allowed us to construct social network graphs of guilds. Every time we saw two characters from the same guild in the same zone (outside the major cities, of course) at the same time, we assumed that they were working together. We would increase their connection weight by 1. Using data spanning thirty days allowed us to create network graphs of guilds—the frequency of interactions between members of that guild. These graphs allowed us to identify the best-connected characters in each guild—the information brokers who bridged different cliques—as well as to quantify how cohesive or fragmented a guild was. In one of our papers, we explored whether we could predict a guild's survival in six months based on its current guild metrics. We found that several of the top predictors were related to diversity. Certainly, a large guild is more likely to survive than a small guild, but what also mattered is having cohesive cliques spread across the range of levels. Because players are constantly getting tired of the game and quitting, the key to a guild's success is in being able to fill those vacant positions rapidly. A guild with only high-level players has difficulty dealing with the turnover, whereas the presence of several cohorts leveling up guarantees long-term guild stability. A vacant slot can be filled with someone who is already familiar with the guild's culture and leaders.[1]

The Magic Box

This early work in *World of Warcraft* data—even with just eight variables—made me realize how special virtual worlds are for social science research. The game can record everything you say, everything you do, and everyone you've talked to and interacted with, no matter where you are in the virtual world. There is nothing near this degree of surveillance in the physical world.

But a more important and subtle point is that many behaviors are already instrumented in a virtual world. Even if we could record every person's behaviors in the physical world, tracking everyone with a video camera, we would still need additional algorithms or manual coding to interpret the recorded behaviors. In an online game, the ambiguity is reduced. Attacking or healing in a game requires specific commands and buttons. In the physical world, someone would need to decode behavior manually: Was that friendly wrestling or a vicious assault?

And all this tracking happens continuously, whenever a player logs into a virtual world. When we run an experiment in a laboratory or ask people to fill out a personality survey, we get snapshot data— how they behaved or what they thought in one moment in time. In a virtual world, we can generate rich longitudinal profiles of how people behave over weeks and months. There are two other important differences between virtual worlds and our current tools such as laboratories and surveys. First, we're not asking people how they might behave in a hypothetical situation or to self-report their preferences. Instead of taking their accounts at face value, we can track their actions directly. Second, unlike being in a psychology lab or filling out a survey, there is no researcher scrutinizing the participant's every action. Most players are not conscious of the game's unobtrusive tracking system because it occurs entirely behind the scenes, silently.

There is nothing in the standard toolset of psychology that even approaches the ability of virtual worlds to gather data on human behavior. Instead of being limited by our ability to bring a few dozen (coerced or bribed) undergraduate students into a physical lab room, we now have access to longitudinal behavioral data from hundreds of thousands of people. And although online gamers are not fully representative of the general population, they are much more diverse than undergraduate students from introductory psychology classes.

But even in 2006 with the PARC PlayOn data and four published papers, we were still quite far from this vision. By relying on server-side data collected with our census add-on, we had information only about characters, not players. We knew nothing about the gender, age, or personality of the players behind the characters. Even though we knew that most players had multiple characters, there was no way to determine that player-character mapping from the server-side data alone. There was also no easy way to survey the players we were tracking because we didn't have their contact information, and it would have been too time-consuming (and suspicion-provoking) to approach them individually in the game. We were close, yet still so far.

Dividing Nature

Although we frequently see portrayals of psychologists on TV and in movies, what those actors do on the screen bears little resemblance to what research psychologists actually do in their work. Portrayals of psychologists tend to focus on clinical psychology and psychiatry—talking to people on couches or prescribing pills to treat mental conditions. Magazines and Facebook apps focus on personality tests. Such portrayals imply that psychology is a science of divination. The psychologist on TV asks the female protagonist about her day and then magically figures out that she has secretly been in love with her adopted brother all her life. And the conceit of personality tests is that taking a few minutes filling out a few innocuous questions somehow lets a magazine know you better than yourself.

In my second-year psychology sequence in college, our professor told us that personality psychology is the closest we would get to what we likely, but incorrectly, thought psychology was about. Personality psychologists certainly conduct studies and run lots of statistics, but at the heart of the research area is the question of how we define and measure personality—the set of interesting individual differences that remain stable over time. Dividing nature is always a contentious business. How do we categorize ethnicities in a census? What are the appropriate checkboxes for sexual orientation? The same is true for personality. It is not hard to see how different psychologists might develop a fondness for certain personality assessment tools over others. This might be because they played a role in the development of a certain taxonomy or their adviser had a preference for one scale over another. Of course, researchers may have empirical reasons for preferring one scale, but not every researcher will agree with those reasons. And there is no grand arbiter of personality scales, so for many decades, psychologists freely developed and published their own personality scales.

Books appeared that collated these disparate scales for easier reference. One popular compilation from 1991 that many psychology researchers have on their reference shelves is *Measures of Personality and Social Psychological Attitudes*. As a sampling of the book's contents, there are eleven different scales for self-esteem, ten different scales for shyness and anxiety, twenty-one different scales for depression and loneliness, and twenty-nine different scales for alienation. The California Psychological Inventory divided personality into thirty-three factors; the Personality Factor Questionnaire divided it into sixteen; the Jackson Personality Inventory divided it into fifteen. Oliver John and Sanjay Srivastava, personality psychologists at UC Berkeley and the University of Oregon, respectively, described this earlier era of personality psychology as a "Babel of concepts and scales" in which researchers were "faced with a bewildering array of personality scales . . . with little guidance and no overall rationale at hand."[2]

A solution emerged in the mid-1980s that began to unify the field of personality psychology. To be more accurate, this approach re-emerged when research from the 1930s came back into vogue after a paradigm shift. The solution hinged on the lexical hypothesis, the assumption that everyday language already captures the most salient personality traits. Any socially relevant trait would find a place in the vocabulary of the people speaking that language. Thus psychologists turned to dictionaries and English texts to extract hundreds of personality-relevant terms. They created large inventories and asked thousands of study participants to rate how well each trait described them. The psychologists' task then was to understand how these terms clustered statistically. By the early 1990s, multiple studies had confirmed that this multitude of English adjectives and phrases could be cleanly divided into five factors. Reliable scales were developed for these factors, and additional studies have shown that they are cross-culturally valid. These personality factors are known as the Big Five, and this personality framework is the current gold standard in personality psychology research.[3]

These five factors form the acronym OCEAN. *Openness to Experience* measures a person's intellectual curiosity, appreciation for art, creativity, and preference for novelty. People with high scores on Openness are more likely to enjoy going to museums and joining in philosophical discussions and to have unconventional ideas and beliefs. People with low scores on Openness are more practical and down-to-earth and more likely to be conventional and traditional. *Conscientiousness* measures self-discipline, organization, planning, and a sense of duty. People who score high on this factor are usually prepared, plan things in advance, and pay attention to details. People who score low on this factor tend to be spontaneous, don't mind a bit of chaos in their lives, and may be perceived by others as disorganized. *Extra-version* measures activity level and the desire to seek out stimulation in social settings. People who score high on this factor enjoy large crowds and being the center of attention, and they have no trouble starting a conversation with strangers. People who score low on this factor avoid social situations, are quiet and reserved, and in general keep in the background. *Agreeableness* measures compassion and coop-eration. People who score high on this factor sympathize with oth-ers' feelings, take time to help others, and are interested in other people's problems. People who score low on this factor tend to be more self-interested, competitive, even antagonistic, and in general suspicious and untrusting of others. *Neuroticism* measures emotional stability and the tendency to experience negative emotions. People who score high on this factor are vulnerable to stress, anxiety, and depression. They are easily upset. People who score low on this fac-tor tend to be calm, emotionally stable, and relaxed.

Ever since the Big Five emerged and became standardized, many researchers have explored how these personality traits are expressed in everyday life. It turns out that personality assessments by complete strangers even after a brief interaction are moderately accurate. Fur-thermore, people tend to use the same cues to infer personality traits. For example, in a study that videotaped strangers getting acquainted, researchers found that people with high Extraversion spoke louder and with more enthusiasm and were more expressive with their gestures. As another example, people with high Conscientiousness wore more formal clothing and were less likely to use rapid body movements. These studies of face-to-face interactions led other re-searchers to wonder whether personality can be inferred from the spaces we inhabit. Personality psychologist Sam Gosling and his colleagues at the University of Texas examined how personality is expressed in people's bedrooms and offices. They found that people with high Conscientiousness had well-lit, neat, and well-organized bedrooms. And people with high Openness to Experience had more varied books and magazines.[4]

These findings also extend to online interactions. Moderately accurate personality impressions can be formed based on an individual's personal website, Facebook profile, email messages, blog posts, and even email address—the smallest slice of online identity expression possible. For example, in terms of a person's blog posts, people with high Agreeableness were more likely to use words related to family and happy emotions (for example, *happy, joy*). And people with high Conscientiousness were more likely to use words related to achievement. Thus, the Big Five isn't just a theoretical framework of personality. These personality traits are also readily expressed when we interact with other people and the world around us. This means that the behavioral traces we leave behind—the blog posts we make, the way we speak, or how often we gesture—are cues that can be used to infer our personalities.[5]

But does personality get expressed in virtual worlds? Given that the average online gamer spends more than twenty hours a week in virtual worlds in which all their actions are tracked, there should be a wealth of digital behavioral cues to find. On the other hand, virtual worlds are different from everyday life precisely in that players are actively encouraged to not be themselves. When people write emails for work or to their friends, their words and identities are rooted in a shared physical reality, and thus it makes sense that their personalities are expressed. You're writing an email as yourself, not as a Night Elf shadow priest. But when we're in a fantasy world where people are in nonhuman bodies doing nonhuman things, are all bets off? In a world in which you can be a gnomish priest resurrecting the dead using magical light rays, does the fantasy break the linkage between personality and behavior?

Quelling Pandora's Box

In 2007, the balance between data access and third parties changed yet again. Blizzard released the Armory for *World of Warcraft*, a website that allows you to look up any active character playing the game. For each character, the Armory catalogs thousands of statistics and achievements. And this list has kept growing with the updates over the years. Currently, the Armory provides over 3,500 variables for each active character, updated daily. These publicly accessible variables cover a broad range of behaviors in *World of Warcraft*: progress through high-level dungeons, combat skill specializations, number of vanity pets owned, frequency and nature of deaths (for example, by drowning or by falling from high places), and even the exact number of virtual hugs given over a character's career. It is an unbelievable treasure trove of data.

Certainly, there is commercial value in the server-side data, but the earlier experiment with add-on scripting created a thriving community of *modders*—gamers developing in-game tools, usually for free. Hundreds of add-ons were developed, many of which were updated diligently with each game patch. The modding community enhanced engagement by allowing gamers to tweak the game interface to their specific play styles. By observing the download counts of the add-ons, it also allowed Blizzard to understand the player community's needs. More than once Blizzard added game functionality that was previously available only with an add-on. If anything was lost with sharing the game data, it was more than made up for with the free programming labor and marketing research generated by the player community. The Armory seemed to expand on this philosophy. The website enhances player engagement by making it easy for new players to understand how elite players are optimizing their equipment and abilities, quickly check a guild candidate's résumé, or figure out what upgrades are available for a character's current equipment. Different websites use the Armory data to create detailed census reports, prevalence of specific classes or specializations in player-versus-player rankings, and the progress of elite guilds in the high-end content. The data sharing created a thriving player community around the game as well as increased the engagement with the game itself.

The Armory also dramatically changed how we could collect data from *World of Warcraft*. Now we could collect data from characters regardless of what server they were on and whether they were currently online. And instead of 7 variables, we now had access to over 3,500. The Armory also solved the problem of linking in-game data with survey data on demographics and personality. We could track census data from an entire server, but there was no easy way to survey those players afterward. The flipside also wouldn't have worked. Say we surveyed players and asked for their active characters. When we were using the old census add-on, there was no easy way to track a random set of characters because they were spread across over two hundred available *World of Warcraft* servers. The cycling time, required to read information on all the servers before repeating, would be so high that, during peak hours, we would miss many characters. With the Armory, it was trivial to access data from a random set of characters, no matter what server they were on. This meant that we could collect survey data from players first and then go to the Armory to access their character data.

In 2009, with the help of a government grant, this was exactly what my colleagues and I at PARC, where I was now a full-time researcher, set out to do. Our team first created an automated collection tool for the Armory. With the infrastructure in place, we collected survey data from more than a thousand *World of Warcraft* players. Apart from demographic and personality information, we asked the players to list their active characters in the game. We then let the Armory data collection accumulate in-game metrics for six months.

Somewhere in those six months it dawned on the team that we were about to be deluged with data. Even when we had just 7 variables in the early PlayOn study, it took us two years to analyze the data. In the new study, we had 1,040 players, each with on average three characters, each of which generated over 3,500 variables per day over a six-month period. In the field of data mining, one well-known saying is "Garbage in, garbage out." Researchers have many tools that allow them to click a few buttons to create attractive graphs and charts, but unless they are feeding these tools meaningful data, the pretty graphs are useless. In 2012, Dmitry Nozhnin, head of analytics at online games publisher Innova, described his experience analyzing data from the online game *Aion*. He was interested in understanding why some players left the game early. Using analytic tools to build complex models, he was able to predict whether a player was about to quit the game, but Nozhnin lamented that even "knowing with very high accuracy when a player will leave, I still don't have a clue why she will leave."[6]

As the PARC team peered into the growing database of Armory data, we were aware of the risk of falling into an abyss of uninterpretable metrics. If Extraversion were correlated with owning a particular set of swords or visiting a particular zone, what does that actually mean? The statistical connection between different variables does not come with an explanation for why they are connected. This is the issue Nozhnin encountered. Moreover, a correlation between two variables does not imply that one caused the other. In fact, the correlation may be caused by a third variable that isn't measured or accounted for. For example, people with bigger feet have bigger brains, but bigger feet do not cause bigger brains. This is because as children get older, both their feet and brains grow larger. The connection between foot size and brain size is coincidental.

A more problematic issue concerned the game variables: many were hopelessly confounded with frequency of gameplay and character progression. Imagine that Frank and I both play *World of Warcraft*. I have a level 80 character—that is, a very high-level character—and Frank has a level 80 and a level 1 character. If we take the average of all the variables for each player, then Frank is unfairly penalized for having a level 1 character. His level 1 character's combat and achievement metrics drag down his overall average. Even if we both have just one character each—say I have a level 40 character and Frank has a level 80 character—we'd still have a problem. Metrics in *World of Warcraft* do not progress linearly; there are sudden, uneven, and exponential gains at certain levels in the game that make it difficult to compare our metrics. If Frank has made 800 player kills at level 80 and I have made 10 player kills at level 40, is Frank really more aggressive than I am, or is it just that level 80 characters have easier access to large numbers of player kills?

We began to develop strategies to create meaningful variables from this morass of data. One was to create conceptually meaningful aggregates. It is impossible to interpret what stepping into any one particular zone means, but the percentage of all zones visited maps to a psychologically meaningful concept of exploration. In short, we tried as much as possible to create variables that came with explanations built in. For the problem of variable confounds, we used multiple normalization strategies. Consider the fact that a player's total amount of healing done in the game is hopelessly confounded with their character level and frequency of playing, but the ratio of healing done against damage done produces a preference metric for healing.

We developed a dozen such strategies to create meaningful variables from the data. And when we examined the connections between real-world personality and in-game behaviors, we found that personality was indeed expressed in *World of Warcraft*. More important, these in-game behaviors aligned with the personality trait definitions.

Players with high Extraversion prefer group activities and are more likely to participate in large dungeon raids. Players with low Extraversion prefer solitary activities such as cooking, fishing, and questing. Players with high Agreeableness give out more virtual hugs, cheers, and waves, preferring noncombat activities such as exploration and crafting. Players with low Agreeableness prefer the combat and antagonistic elements of the game. They enjoy killing other players, die more often, and participate in more duels and arena matches. Players with high Conscientiousness enjoy collecting things in the game, whether this is accumulating vanity pets or travel mounts (for example, horses, griffons). They also enjoy the self-discipline required to advance in the cooking and fishing professions. On the other hand, players with low Conscientiousness are more likely to die from falling from high places. Players with high

Openness to Experience have more active characters, are more likely to have characters on multiple servers, and spend more time exploring the game world. Players with low Openness to Experience prefer the traditional combat elements of the game, focusing on dungeons and raiding.

Neuroticism was the only trait that did not have a clear correspondence with in-game behaviors. Nevertheless, the predominant pattern of correspondence between real-world personality and in-game behavior is striking. Neither the overt fantasy nor the constant invitations to reinvent ourselves drown out our personalities. Even when we take on virtual bodies, our personalities are expressed in online games.[7]

The Digital Panopticon

We also used machine learning tools to see if we could extract simple rules that could predict someone's demographic attributes based on his or her in-game behaviors. The rules for predicting gender had surprisingly high accuracies. If you play a male character for more than 61 percent of your total playing time, there is a 94 percent chance that you are male in real life. And if you have no male characters and have given out more than eighty-nine hugs, there is a 93 percent chance that you are female in real life. As Charles Duhigg reports in his book The Power of Habit, the retail chain Target used similar predictive tools to infer whether female shoppers were pregnant based on their shopping behavior. By accurately making this inference before a baby is born (and before the public birth record invites a flood of advertisements from retailers), Target would be able to capitalize on a moment in a woman's life when her routines and habits change because of a significant life event. By sending advertisements at this critical juncture, Target hoped to create new shopping habits. Target's algorithm was so successful that they figured out that a teenage girl was pregnant before she had told her parents; they were tipped off when Target addressed congratulatory coupons for baby clothes and cribs to the pregnant teen. The Proteus Paradox reveals psychological tools in virtual worlds that have a great synergy. Virtual worlds not only provide novel methods for psychological control, they also provide the means to perfectly tailor those manipulations based on an individual's attitudes, demographics, attributes, and personality.[8]

Peter Steiner's 1993 cartoon in the New Yorker captured the promise of freedom and anonymity that the Internet once offered: "On the Internet, nobody knows you're a dog." But our era of big data—especially as more data are captured and at finer-grain resolutions—flips this premise around. Our behaviors online, in virtual worlds, and when using smart mobile devices allow others to make accurate inferences about who we are and what we like. On the Internet, everybody knows you're a dog. And as marketers and advertisers compete over this growing flood of data, the facts they learn about each of us are likely to become more and more unsettling. Pregnancy may be a celebratory occasion, but what about the onset of diabetes, an impending divorce, or impending unemployment? These retailers not only have data from you, they also have data from your friends, children, spouse, and employer. What happens when a retail store knows that your spouse is planning to leave you before you do? Furthermore, the true risk may not be in accurate predictions but, rather, in inaccurate predictions. Target may send you shopping coupons if they think you are pregnant, but what might law enforcement agencies do if they think you are committing a crime? On an April morning in 2012, a Kansas family found out when a police squad armed with assault rifles stormed their house. The family believes they were targeted because they had purchased hydroponic supplies to grow plants indoors. The police squad did not find marijuana even after a drug-sniffing dog was brought in to help, but they did find six plants in the basement: three tomatoes, one melon, and two butternut squash.[9]

We are living in a world in which a digital escapist fantasy and a surveillance state refer to the same thing. Media scholar Mark Andrejevic uses the phrase "digital enclosure" to refer to this rapidly growing phenomenon of users freely submitting to enhanced surveillance in order to gain access to a digital network or community—whether it is Gmail, Facebook, or virtual worlds. Not only do virtual worlds provide unprecedented powers of surveillance, they also provide unprecedented executive powers. In January 2005, many *World of Warcraft* players became disgruntled with the announced changes to the warrior class. In addition to complaining on web forums, they staged an in-game protest. These disgruntled players created level 1 gnome warriors on the Thunderlord server, stripped down save for their loincloths, and protested on the bridge in the Dwarven city of Ironforge. Soon afterward, many of those players found their game account locked, with the following message displayed on their log-in screen: "This World of Warcraft account has been suspended— Please check the registered email address of this account for further information." It is easy to create and customize virtual characters. It is equally easy to delete virtual characters; our digital bodies do not decompose and do not require elaborate disposal methods. Existence comes and goes at the click of a button.[10]

CHAPTER 10 CHANGING THE RULES

> Cyberspace does not guarantee its own freedom but instead carries an
> extraordinary potential for control. . . . Architecture is a kind of law: it
> determines what people can and cannot do.
>
> Lawrence Lessig, *Code*

If you were to lose your wallet in New York City, what's the chance
that someone would return it with the cash intact? As a social experiment, Mark West, a law professor at the University of Michigan,
dropped twenty wallets, each containing $20 and an identification
card that listed a telephone number, in Midtown Manhattan. Of these
twenty dropped wallets, six were returned with cash intact and another two without the cash. West conducted the same experiment in
Shinjuku, a business and shopping district in Tokyo. Of the twenty
dropped wallets, seventeen were returned, all with cash intact. West
also dropped hundreds of cell phones in similar experiments, with
comparable differences between the United States and Japan. After
the devastating tsunami in 2011, Japanese citizens turned over a stunning $48 million in loose cash—found in purses or paper envelopes
among the debris—to local authorities. Authorities also collected an
additional $30 million from recovered safes.[1]

Without knowing anything else about Japan, it might be easy to
assume that collectivist Asian cultures instill a greater sense of honesty and altruism in their citizens, whereas individualist cultures like
the United States encourage a finders-keepers mentality. But when

West interviewed the participants in his experiment, he found the opposite. Of the New Yorkers who returned wallets and cell phones, 91 percent explained their actions by invoking altruism or honesty. One interviewee stressed that "I'm an honest person"; another said, "I couldn't live with myself if I kept your money." In contrast, only 18 percent of the people in Japan who returned the wallets invoked altruism or honesty. Instead, 84 percent invoked the finders-keepers mentality, providing such answers as, "If the owner doesn't claim it, I have a right to it," and "I want the reward money."

Japan has a very effective and widely understood legal framework around returning lost objects. Any found object can be turned in at *kôbans*—small neighborhood police stations that are ubiquitous throughout Japan. Two carrots and one stick incentivize this behavior. The first carrot is that owners have to pay the finder a percentage of the object's value if they claim the object; this percentage ranges between 5 and 25 percent depending on the type of property and the circumstances. The second carrot is that if no one claims the object after six months, the finder gets to keep the object. There is also one stick; a finder who misappropriates the object has committed embezzlement and is subject to a $1,200 fine and imprisonment of up to one year.

Rules can powerfully influence social behavior. What is most striking about the difference between the New York and Tokyo return rates is that plain altruism and honesty perform only about one third as well as a good set of rules.

In the physical world, there are a large number of immutable laws of nature—gravity, thermodynamics, electromagnetism—that we have no control over. These natural laws touch every aspect of our daily lives: under what lighting conditions our eyes can see, how far our voices travel when we whisper or shout, how many people can fit in a room, and what happens when we die.

In virtual worlds, a programmer has to define every law of nature. In the original *Dark Age of Camelot*, you could shout a message only when you were inside a city zone. In the original *EverQuest*, you couldn't walk through another player's avatar, but you can do so in *World of Warcraft*. In *Star Wars Galaxies*, you couldn't teleport yourself from one location to another—you had to always manually navigate there yourself, but teleportation is available via skills and magical objects in *World of Warcraft*. And these rules change how people interact with each other, often in unintended ways. In the original *EverQuest*, in which you couldn't walk through another avatar, pairs or groups of players could block the zone entrance and watch as a train of monsters massacred bystanders desperately trying to exit the zone. In *Star Wars Galaxies*, malicious shopkeepers could entrap unwary customers by placing a piece of furniture in front of the door.

Programmers design many of these game mechanics for the functional aspects of gameplay, but game mechanics are also rules that can unintentionally change how we relate and interact with each other. In this sense, virtual worlds are the grandest social experiments that have ever existed. Any variable in the world, in the rules, in the way players interact with each other, can be infinitely tweaked. For example, how might society organize differently if people always came back to life when they died?

The Price of Immortality

In online games, your character dies when its health drops to zero as a result of such things as combat damage, slow-acting poisons, or falling from great heights. The consequences of dying then depend on which game you are playing. In many games, the character's body (that is, the corpse) remains at the location of death and the player (in spirit form) has to travel back to the corpse to resurrect the character. In some games, like *World of Warcraft*, your weapons and armor are slightly damaged when you die and you need to spend game currency to repair that damage. Other games apply an experience penalty after each death. For example, in *EverQuest II* and *City of Heroes*, you accrue a percentage penalty to experience earned—for example, you earn only half the normal experience for the next one thousand experience points. In the original *EverQuest*, characters lost accrued experience when they died, and a character could even lose his or her level by dying. In the most extreme cases, death actually means death, and the game erases the character. This mechanic was present in very specific scenarios in *Star Wars Galaxies* and *EverQuest*.

On an abstract level, death penalties are all variants of time penalties (with the exception of the case of complete erasure, or *permadeath*); dying means spending extra time to catch up to where you were, but nothing is lost permanently. Of course, losing accrued experience is subjectively more painful than a temporarily slower experience gain. One of the most striking trends in online games over the past decade is the softening of the death penalty. For example, in early *EverQuest*, you had to run back to your corpse naked. All your equipment stayed with your corpse. And there was a corpse timer. If you couldn't retrieve your corpse in time, your equipment decayed and disappeared. Because players are more likely to die in dangerous places, retrieving a corpse while naked is doubly dangerous and can result in dying again. Death in the early online games was a costly mishap.

You could play for six hours and lose all the progress by dying twice. You could log in and log off with less than you came on with. [*World of Warcraft*, female, 25, describing experience in *EverQuest*]

In contrast, dying in most contemporary online games is almost a lighthearted affair.

I have spent significant time in Dark Age of Camelot, EverQuest II, and Lord of The Rings Online since playing EverQuest classic. . . . In subsequent games, I have found it absolutely does not matter if I die. Really, who cares about some repair bills and some dread, or decreased experience gain for a short time? Running naked after your corpse in a dungeon? Potentially losing all your equipment if your corpse decayed or losing a level? That was a penalty. [*Lord of the Rings Online*, male, 31]

The severe death penalties in earlier online games created a pervasive sense of risk and danger in the world. The *EverQuest* world of Norrath was simply not a safe place to be running around in. Staying alive was a constant concern. In comparison, the contemporary *World of Warcraft* world of Azeroth is like a rubber-padded playground.

I remember working for two weeks in the original EverQuest to get to level 5. I finally got brave and wandered a few hundred yards away from the guards in Kelethin and promptly got lost in the fog. I was soon attacked by several level 8 mobs and died. I've never experienced that level of fear and concern as I searched frantically for my corpse. I currently play World of Warcraft and enjoy it for the most part. However, there is no need to ask for help as the game does 90% of the work for you. In some ways I like that, but at times I really wish someone could come up with a way to recapture the original spark that kept me playing EverQuest for close to five years. [*World of Warcraft*, male, 39, describing earlier experience in *EverQuest*]

It is this shared understanding of the pervasive specter of death that contributed to a higher level of willingness of players to help each other. Norrath was fundamentally a world in which you could not survive alone. Players helped each other because they knew that one day they would be the ones asking for help; building a social support network was key to one's survival in *EverQuest*.

> It was definitely more important to work together when there were death penalties. Finding someone who could rez [resurrect] or summon your corpse, or someone to help you retrieve it was key. People helped others because they knew they themselves would probably need similar help later. [*World of Warcraft*, female, 21, describing experience in *EverQuest*]

> Guilds, even enemy guilds, would help each other recover from bad wipes because they knew that there were occasions when they would need help. This helped to mitigate annoying behavior since you knew you may need to work together at times. [*Vanguard*, male, 42, describing experience in *EverQuest*]

In an earlier survey of *EverQuest* players I ran in 2000, I asked players to describe their most memorable experience from the game. Many players' stories revolved around altruism. The following player narrative exemplifies these stories.

> My primary character is a Cleric, so on one occasion my guild was on a raid in a dungeon area and I came across one player's corpse. This was unusual because of where we were and how deep we were in the dungeon. I sent this person a "tell" to see if she needed a res. She replied and was very excited that I was there to res her. After she gathered her equipment she tried to give me some Platinum pieces, which I refused since I didn't go out of my way to help her . . . I was just there. A month later, my guild was performing another raid and we were wiped out by some unexpected baddies. . . . The person I resurrected happened to be in a group near the beginning of the dungeon where we were wiped out, and before I knew it, most of her guild was there to help clear the dungeon and get our corpses back. I mean about 30

other players went out of their way to come and help my friends out just because I helped one of their friends a month before. I don't know many people who would do that in real life. . . . All I can say is . . . Thank you Ostara. [*EverQuest*, male, 32]

Death was certainly painful in EverQuest, but oddly, it was precisely death that brought people together. The shared crises and aftermath created salient memories for everyone involved. Death was the bright red thread that wove itself through the social fabric of EverQuest.

As much as I hated corpse runs back in old EQ, having to run naked from Fironia Vie to Chardok with a coffin to have my corpse summoned after a raid wipe with my guild was a bonding experience. [*World of Warcraft*, male, 20, describing experience in *EverQuest*]

While I'm glad the severe death penalty has been removed from Ever-Quest, I think it helped my character bond with her friends. I'm still playing with the same folks I met 8 years ago, and we often talk about the dreaded CRs (corpse retrievals) we went through, especially one in Chardok that lasted hours. [*EverQuest*, female, 61]

Saying you will help someone and actually doing it are two different things. EverQuest allowed players to prove themselves trustworthy through their actions. The willingness to spend an hour to help a friend to retrieve a corpse isn't something that can be faked.

To succeed in EverQuest you need to form relationships with people you can trust. The game does a wonderful job of forcing people in this situation. RL [real life] rarely offers this opportunity as technological advances mean we have little reliance on others. [*EverQuest*, male, 29]

In these early online games, as much as everyone was trying to avoid dying, death was actually a bonding experience. Death created debts and then allowed those debts to be repaid over time. Death created deep bonds based on mutual trust.

Weaving the Social Fabric

In older online games like EverQuest, combat occurred at a glacial pace; monsters took minutes to kill and players had time to chat during combat. Contemporary online game designers have streamlined pacing to minimize any downtime. The action is brisk and constant. But downtime performed a valuable social function in the older games. It gave players a chance to talk to each other. In streamlined games, chatting is instead viewed as slowing down the combat (and thus experience gain). In EverQuest, if you didn't chat during the downtime, there was nothing else to do.

> Relationships always seemed more based on the speed of the game and the speed of progress than anything else—EverQuest was so slow and had so much downtime that you had plenty of time to chat, help people in fights, buff passersby and answer questions. In World of Warcraft no one stops to look [because] by the time they have stopped to see if someone needs helps it's probably too late. [World of Warcraft, male, 38]

> I think the total lack of downtime where you rest and relax together before fighting the next challenge lowers your chances of having a good interaction with people. Without those connections, those hooks most people will never ask questions about each other or make commonality discoveries. [EverQuest, male, 35]

As the player in the first narrative notes, the glacial pace of combat in EverQuest also made it more likely that a random passerby could jump in and provide assistance. In games like World of Warcraft, there is much less time to react, to ask for help, and to provide help.

Another game mechanism that has changed a great deal over time is character independence. In the original EverQuest, many crucial or useful abilities were limited to one or two character classes. Binding is one of these abilities. When a character dies in EverQuest, it is teleported back to its bind location. To change your bind location, you must ask a magic user to cast the binding spell on you. Given the hassles of corpse runs, players would rebind themselves frequently as they adventured. Thus, nonmagic users often shouted out for binding when they reached a new zone. The same is true of other spells that dramatically increased traveling time or mana recovery—the shaman's Spirit of Wolf spell and the enchanter's Clarity spell, respectively. And only the wizard class had access to group teleportation spells. In EverQuest, asking other players for these spells was the only way to get many things done in a timely manner.

Compare this with more recent online games, which tend to emphasize character independence. In World of Warcraft, players can bind themselves to any tavern without any help. And there are flight paths and mounts that anyone can use to decrease traveling time. There are also multiple ways of teleporting group members. Dependence on other players in EverQuest encouraged social interaction in two important ways. It provided many opportunities for approaching and talking to someone, often a stranger. And one subtle point bears emphasizing: the more people you have the opportunity to interact with, the more likely your social network will grow. You can't make friends if you never talk to anyone.

> In the old days of EverQuest, people helped people because they had no other way to get help. [World of Warcraft, male, 32]

This created a cultural norm of asking for and providing help to strangers. For example, because Spirit of Wolf was such a valuable traveling aid, shamans were used to being asked to cast it. And enchanters were used to being asked to cast Clarity.

The opposite is true in most contemporary online games. The shift to high levels of character independence—to attract and retain more casual players—means that it is possible to solo the game to the maximum level. While early online games made it mandatory to group up, this mandate has shifted over time to encouragement and, recently, simply to an option. Certainly, players must form dedicated guilds to complete the high-level raids in *World of Warcraft*, but a great deal of the game content can be completed alone or with ad hoc groups.

> The big solo experience that today's MMOs focus at make it easier to log in just for a little while and achieve something, but in my experience it takes away a lot of immersion and bonding to other players / guild / game. [*EverQuest II*, female, 28]

> In general, I think EverQuest required more dependence and community. And heck, you HAD to group to get much of anything done. There was virtually no level-appropriate solo content. Now, a person can actually level all the way to max level in both EverQuest II (although it was not always true of this game) and certainly in Lord of the Rings Online without ever grouping. [*Lord of the Rings Online*, female, 44]

In a world where you never have to ask other players for help and can do everything alone, the social fabric suffers. Asking for help becomes a sign of weakness and incompetence. Personal reputations no longer matter.

> When I started playing World of Warcraft I was amazed with the total lack of respect that people have for each other. It didn't take me long to realize because the game is easy, you don't need to respect anybody or make friends. You can solo to maximum level. You can ninja-loot epics and then just switch servers or even change your name now. In EverQuest you lived by your reputation. I remember an incident where I somehow got under somebody's skin in a group and then I couldn't get a grinding group in Dreadlands for like 3 days. [*Vanguard*, male, 25]

> I keep contacts with former EverQuest companions to this day as we went through thick and thin together. In the new games, notably

World of Warcraft or EverQuest 2, you can hardly agree with people on which server we will play—because who cares; there is no need for real cooperation. [*Vanguard*, male, 39]

In Adam Guettal's musical *The Light in the Piazza*, there is a wonderful moment in the beginning of the second act when the matriarch of a lively Italian family unexpectedly breaks the fourth wall. The orchestration stops abruptly; she turns to the audience and says, "I don't speak English, but I have to tell you what's going on."

> Aiutami means "help me" in Italian
> . . . .
> Risk is everything
> Without risk, there is no drama
> Without drama, there is no "aiutami"
> Without asking for help
> No love! No love!

The pervasive danger in the world of *EverQuest* made asking for help a necessity. Finding players you could trust was a fundamental strategy for survival. And from these unending trials and tribulations, lasting relationships were forged.

In chapter 9, when I describe the historical development of the study of personality traits, I briefly mentioned that research on traits was abandoned in the 1970s and early 1980s. Psychologist Walter Mischel sparked this paradigm shift. Using published research on trait psychology, he pointed out that traits could not predict how a person would behave in a specific situation. Instead, Mischel argued, situations largely shape human behavior and the notion of static personality traits is a myth. Thus, Bob is talkative and gregarious at a party but quiet in the library. And Rachel is nervous when interviewing for a job but calm when watching TV at home. Differences among individuals are thus largely overshadowed by differences across situations. In the decades following Mischel's critique and since trait theory has come back into fashion, researchers like Allan Buss have called for a move toward an interactionist approach—blending trait theory with understanding contextual demands—but as a field, personality psychology has tended to focus on standardizing trait measures.[2]

Mischel's perspective provides a fascinating way of interpreting the social fabric of EverQuest. We're used to thinking of altruism as a personality trait, but altruism can also be a system trait. A community can be designed with rules and mechanisms that engineer altruistic behavior, as seen with the relatively larger percentage of wallet returns in Japan and with the cultural norms that emerged in EverQuest. In the world of EverQuest, altruism was something you needed to exhibit in order to survive in the game. The rules in a virtual world create an invisible scaffold that favors the creation of certain social norms, tacitly dictating how and when players interact. These invisible scaffolds are the social architectures of virtual worlds; they are the ground rules that govern the DNA of the community that emerges.

Information Access

Game developers usually design and control social architectures, but not always. This is because a great deal of the game actually exists outside the virtual world itself. The complexity of rules and abundance of information in online games mean that players frequently encounter quests, items, and game mechanics that they are unfamiliar with. Online gamers spend on average 3.5 hours each week looking for game-related information, another 3.5 hours each week reading or posting on forums. And players who belong to guilds spend another 2.7 hours each week on their guild's website forums or managing guild-related tasks (such as scheduling). Thus, the average online gamer spends about 22 hours in the game each week and an additional 10.8 hours in the meta-game.[3]

In early online games, before the days of game wikis, a great deal of forum activity was devoted to information sharing, but searching for specific information was cumbersome. Different people used different terminology and phrasings, and a player, even after finding the correct thread, would have to scan and read all the posts to find the one with the definitive answer.

Now, the data-sharing initiatives in games like *World of Warcraft* make it possible for gamers to get their hands directly on the information that matters to them. The same data sources that allowed my PARC colleagues and me to study *World of Warcraft* also allowed intrepid developers to create valuable information databases. One of the best-known examples of these efforts was the database Thottbot. There were two parts to Thottbot. The first was a minimalist website where players could go to search for *World of Warcraft* information. The second was an add-on called Cosmos that came with several useful in-game features. But along with Cosmos was a background data logger. Any monster you killed, any item you found, and any quest you were working on were meticulously tracked by the add-on. Players who had installed Cosmos could then periodically upload their data logs to Thottbot.

The things that Cosmos tracked may not seem particularly useful at first glance, but the accumulated data contained a kind of crowd-sourced wisdom. On the Thottbot website, players could type in the name of a quest and see a map showing where the requisite items were located. If the quest involved killing a monster, a map showed the wandering range of the monster and the percentage likelihood that the monster would drop the needed item. Alternatively, players could search for an item and view a sorted list of all the monsters that dropped it or the quests that provided the item as a reward. And each item, quest, and monster had a comments page, allowing players to discuss tricky strategies or confusing parts of a quest. Players have aggregated information on almost every in-game aspect of World of Warcraft that they can search and sort in a unified and easy-to-use website.

Game developers have also provided in-game access to information, and this has tended to increase over the years. You can ask computer-controlled guards in World of Warcraft cities for directions. They then provide a red marker on your map. Many games provide the player with a map of a zone automatically once they step foot in that zone. And a mini-map is always present at the top right corner of the user interface showing a top-down view of the surroundings. This is in stark contrast to earlier games such as EverQuest, which did not provide any maps to players.

> When I was playing EverQuest years ago, there were websites with game info out there, but they were always incomplete. Unlike with World of Warcraft today, I couldn't always find out what I needed to know. . . . But now, you'd be hard-pressed to find any aspect of World of Warcraft that isn't well-documented online somewhere, complete with video footage and everything. [World of Warcraft, female, 33]

Making information accessible might be expected to provide benefits to a community, but by providing a unified information source, databases like Thottbot removed the primary method of gathering information before—by interacting with other human players.

> Personally I think the older games did a better job of forming communities. There wasn't places on line you could go to get all the answers,

you had to ask other players. There was a lot more give and take. [*World of Warcraft*, male, 29]

I much preferred the early days of MMOs when all the information you ever needed wasn't available on a website. It meant players actually worked together, spoke and chatted lots in the general channels about things directly related to the game and helped each other with quests. [*Pirates of the Burning Sea*, female, 38]

In the earlier games, asking someone for help actually benefited both players. The following player narrative is particularly insightful in articulating how the responder also gained something out of the transaction.

Players were more inclined to help each other, I think, because most of the game knowledge resided in the heads of the gamers themselves rather than being documented somewhere. So it was somewhat a source of pride to be *able* to answer someone's obscure question. It proved you were a seasoned player and made you seem like a nice guy. [*World of Warcraft*, female, 33, describing experience in *EverQuest*]

With the availability of information, the calculus of asking for help changed. There was no longer a need to ask for information, and no need to provide information. Publicly asking for help with a quest or a location became anachronistic and a mark of ignorance.

I have seen many players getting told to look up simple quest directions on thottbot.com and at the same time being insulted for being a "noob." [*World of Warcraft*, male, 29]

Standard responses to questions in the general channels online are "look it up" or "check thottbot." [*World of Warcraft*, male, 33]

Of course, this also changes the social fabric of the community. The fewer people you talk to and interact with, the fewer relationships that form. It bears repeating that you can easily play *World of Warcraft* and level up to the maximum level without ever talking to anyone. Indeed, my PARC colleagues and I have found that until players reach the maximum level, they spend most of their time playing alone.[4]

> These online resources do affect the number of relationships formed in-game. Without them, the player offering help will probably have to explain things to the one asking for it, but with it he'll just give a link. [*Tabula Rasa*, male, 20]

> If people were more willing to answer questions, it would be a great conversation starter and there would be more friendships forming. [*World of Warcraft*, female, 26]

These third-party databases and add-ons not only provide access to information outside of the game, but some add-ons even provide dynamic, in-game assistance. QuestHelper is a good example of this. This add-on analyzes all the active quests that a player has and calculates the most efficient path to minimize completion time. Quest-related items and monsters are marked on the map to guide the player along. By removing all the unknowns, all the imprecise information, and all the mystery, these information sources also gradually removed the sense of adventure in more recent online games.

> Maps, databases, etc. have taken the mystery out of playing. While it saves time and minimizes frustration, I think in doing so, they've also killed a big part of what makes the games exciting. Yes, it's nice to see what the quest reward is going to be, but it removes any surprises you might have had. Adventuring, finding things out for yourself, discovering things, etc. is a huge part of what makes games fun and interesting. It saddens me that to really enjoy a game, you have to make a conscious effort to avoid or ignore all the tips and info available. [*Lord of the Rings Online*, female, 40]

I think Thottbott has created more of a Task-oriented game world. I have a quest, look up where to go and what to do, complete, get a new quest. As a result the "discovery" aspect of the game has lessened significantly. [*World of Warcraft*, male, 42]

Instead of a fantasy world where players experience adventures, the game becomes a task list—a graphical, action-packed task list, but one requiring fewer problem-solving skills and less creativity. The game is no longer about unraveling mysteries, exploring, or meeting fellow adventurers but about completing assignments efficiently. As described in chapter 4, the game becomes a work platform. And in this quest to complete tasks as efficiently as possible, other people become irrelevant distractions.

> If you met someone in a mid-level zone while questing, chances are you'd pass them by. You're on a quest and your mission is to get it done, probably ASAP. They're probably thinking the same thing and you'll pass right by. Who knows what interesting conversations you could've had. If you happen to meet doing the same quest, you'll probably join up for a while, slaughter a few minions together, then part ways. I could swear that about 75 percent of people you meet randomly like this will be so intent on completing a quest and moving on to get the next quest are so incredibly focused on it, barely a word will be exchanged between you. There's such an incredibly selfish behaviour when it comes to questing to GET IT DONE that it becomes bigger than anything else. [*World of Warcraft*, male, 20]

Even when you need a group to kill a quest monster, the group finishes and disbands almost as soon as it forms. These games turn "friends" into fungible, disposable resources. It really doesn't matter who that somebody is as long as there is some *body* there. The "massively multiplayer" description of these games is a surprising misnomer. Certainly guilds provide social stability, but guilds become a necessity only when players reach the higher levels. MIT's Sherry

Turkle has seen this same pattern play out in our fast-paced, gadget-embracing lives. In her book *Alone Together*, she writes, "We are increasingly connected to each other but oddly more alone; in intimacy, new solitudes." The machines and systems that offer to help us often take something away when we're not looking.[5]

The Give and Take

There are of course many other mechanisms in online games that might influence the communities and social norms that form, but the three we've explored in this chapter show that the mechanisms in any particular game are but one set out of a wide range of possible designs. What is more, game mechanics not only change how we play the game but also change how we treat other players. At first glance, the rules of death, independence, and the accessibility of information should have nothing to do with altruism and relationship formation, but it turns out they do. They influence how likely players are to ask for help and whether help is offered. They influence whether we see other players as valuable allies or disposable resources. We tend to think of traits like altruism as individual traits, but altruism can be part of the social architecture of virtual worlds. Whether the city guard gives us directions in a game isn't something we would have expected to alter how we treat each other. As with face-morphing and doppelgängers, the sources of change in the Proteus Paradox are often unintuitive and beyond our control.

Life in *EverQuest* was certainly not all campfire kumbayas. The severe death penalties and pervasive risks created both heroes and cowards. There were always strangers who were willing to help you, but strangers ready to take advantage of you as well.

We had a group of 5 in one of the Gnoll dungeons. A caster (I believe it was a wizard) asked if he could join us. Since we were full & he was a good 10 levels higher than us we politely declined. He then complained for a bit & went invisible. We forgot about him & proceeded to start fighting. We ended up having a large number of adds & most of us were very close to dying so we were running for the zone line. I was a couple steps from the zone when the wizard decided to cast an area effect spell & kill almost all of us. It was an extremely rude & childish thing to do just because we wouldn't let him group with us. [EverQuest, female, 27]

Clearly not all EverQuest strangers were helpful. If anything, what EverQuest guaranteed was an emotional rollercoaster. There were indelible peaks and gut-wrenching lows. In contrast, more recent online games like World of Warcraft offer a stable, mild buzz. If EverQuest were a suspenseful postapocalyptic survival horror movie, then World of Warcraft would be a predictable romantic comedy. But while EverQuest never promised that everyone you met would be kind, it did promise that everyone would walk away with memorable stories and that many would find friendships that outlived the game itself.

Of course, none of this makes World of Warcraft a bad game by any stretch of the imagination. World of Warcraft has outsold EverQuest more than twenty times over—having 12 million players versus 450,000 at their respective peaks. By implementing mechanisms that favored a more solo, casual play style, World of Warcraft dramatically increased the market size of the genre. But as I've described in this chapter, these mechanisms likely also dramatically changed the communities and social norms that formed. The mechanisms that make the game easier to get into probably also make the game easier to leave. Independence cuts both ways.

I often find myself reflecting on my online gaming experiences.

The salient memories I have tend to come from earlier games—trekking cross-continent in *EverQuest* or selling pharmaceutical supplies in *Star Wars Galaxies*, whereas memories from the more recent games tend to be hazy. I'm sure I suffer from some nostalgic rose-tinting, but as fond as my memories are of the dangerous worlds of earlier online games, I doubt I would be able to stomach them now; the accepted tedium of the past would feel like torture after the casual independence of more recent online games. And I think that once gamers become habituated to the rubber-padding, it becomes difficult to wean them off of it. You can't put the genie back in the bottle. In this sense, the games we have played limit the games that can be made. It's like feeding children ice cream and then hoping they will then want carrots. But this race to casualness has resulted in online games sharing a certain amount of interchangeable blandness. In online games, when death is meaningless, so too is life. I'm not suggesting that we want virtual worlds to be filled with harsh tedium, but I'm not sure lonely antagonism is where we want to be either. The question is whether gamers are too habituated to casual online games for us to reach a middle ground.

In chapter 8, I cataloged the many ways in which our avatars can unexpectedly change how we think and behave. But the influence of avatars in fact starts at a much more fundamental level. As a final example of the Proteus Paradox, I describe in this chapter how avatars change how we think about virtual worlds and the worlds we end up creating.

In the media and pop culture, the phrases "virtual world" and "virtual reality" are sometimes used interchangeably, but in the field of computer science, "virtual reality" has a specific meaning. Research in virtual reality is about creating immersive, digital environments that are sufficiently realistic to make you feel as if you were really in a different physical place. Not just a computer screen with a keyboard and mouse, but an actual digital world you can physically walk around in and interact with—the *Star Trek* holodeck made real. Helmets with position tracking, goggles with tiny display screens, and gloves with tactile feedback are innovations from this line of research. Ivan Sutherland developed the first virtual reality system in the 1960s, and these tools became commercially available (though prohibitively expensive for mass market adoption) in the mid-1980s when Jaron Lanier founded the virtual reality gear seller VPL Research.[1]

John Perry Barlow, one of the founding members of the Electronic Frontier Foundation, documented his first experience in one of Lanier's early virtual reality systems: "Suddenly I don't have a body anymore. . . . The closest analog to Virtual Reality in my experience is psychedelic, and, in fact, cyberspace is already crawling with delighted acid heads. . . . Nothing could be more disembodied or insensate than the experience of cyberspace. It's like having had your everything amputated." Barlow titled this article "Being in Nothingness." The connection between hippies and virtual reality is not intuitive, but the counterculture movement was fascinated with using technology to create immersive experiences of shared, disembodied consciousness. This is the common denominator behind the counterculture's embrace of LSD, strobe lights, Day-Glo paint, and the nascent virtual reality systems; they are all tools with which to transcend the physical limitations of the human body. To Barlow, what was unique and revelatory about cyberspace was that you didn't need to have a body.[2]

Neither virtual worlds nor virtual reality has taken this path. Much of the current research in the field of virtual reality focuses on creating experiences that replicate the physical world as faithfully as possible—simulating physical bodies in physical places with voice actors and high-resolution graphics. For example, the Institute of Creative Technologies creates immersive military training simulations. In one of these exercises, a trainee is immersed in a 3D virtual simulation in the streets of Bosnia where his Humvee has just accidentally injured a young boy. The boy's mother is angrily confronting the trainee in a foreign language. The goal of the exercise is to train soldiers for cross-cultural interactions. And of course, before you can actually play an online game you first have to create your own avatar. If anything, we are obsessed with our virtual bodies. As I noted in chapter 8, there are more than 150 sliders to customize your avatar in *Second Life*.[3]

In 2003, Byron Reeves and Leighton Read chatted at a swim meet—both their daughters swam competitively in high school. Reeves was a professor at Stanford University in the department of communication, and Read was a partner at a Palo Alto venture capital firm. "Poolside discussions quickly led to exciting brainstorming sessions with colleagues we cajoled into helping. Eventually, a small group hatched a first project—a conference about games and work." This quickly led to the creation of a startup named Seriosity. In a nutshell, their mission was to figure out how to harness the appeal of games to make corporate work more fun. To their credit, this was years before the word *gamification*—now used to describe this application of game design in serious work—came into popular usage.[4]

In early 2004, they brought me onboard as a game consultant, and we quickly hired gamers from Stanford University to help us explore this space. We ran through many team exercises to map out the possibilities—the gamer students showed us how raiding worked in *World of Warcraft*, Reeves and Read set up business case competitions, and we experimented with prototypes in *Second Life*. In one particularly disastrous and memorable exercise, we held a business meeting in *Second Life*. Unlike online games, *Second Life* is a virtual sandbox with no game goals. Every user can create new content in the world—for example, a custom-designed virtual mansion with guests greeted by a scripted, virtual robot.

And so we found ourselves in a virtual meeting room that we had paid a *Second Life* designer to create for us. There were virtual chairs around a virtual table in front of a virtual screen, where we would display doubly virtual PowerPoint slides. As we navigated toward the chairs and sat down, some of us noticed that the avatar heads in front of us blocked our views of the screens. Unlike the real world, there was no easy way to tilt your head. And because the virtual chairs were bolted to particular spots on the ground, there was also no way to move around once you were seated. Now, Second Life does allow you to control your camera independent of your avatar's position, but this was too confusing for people who were using Second Life for the first time. And so we spent about fifteen minutes trying unsuccessfully to solve a problem that we solve spontaneously and immediately in the physical world. Some team members ended up not using the virtual chairs and had their avatars stand on the side of the room during the entire slide presentation. I remember sitting in my virtual chair, silently pondering the elephant in the room: If our virtual bodies never get tired from standing up, why do we need virtual chairs in the first place?

Once you have bodies, social norms from the physical world come into play. Avatar bodies need to be clothed, their hair styled. It would be distracting to have a business meeting with bald and naked colleagues. Clothing invites additional social norms. In the same way that appearances matter in the physical world, they matter in the digital world. Few want to wear a potato sack when others have fashionable and form-fitting ensembles, especially when those stylish clothes might be bought for mere pennies. In Second Life, hundreds of stores popped up that sold brand-name clothing knockoffs, dramatic hairstyles, and even impossibly sculpted, athletic bodies. Given the affordability of this decadence, virtual worlds can encourage a meticulous scrutiny and obsessive fascination with our virtual bodies.

The founder of Second Life, Philip Rosedale, has reflected on this "sum of all our dreams":

> It's a world that is what they wanted and it's a world of everyone's aspi-
> rations. . . . It's a world that has bathrooms, because we value bath-
> rooms. It's a world that has Ferraris and Rolexes. . . . What we all want
> is a sort of Frank-Lloyd-Wright cantilevered house on that cliff [in] Los
> Angeles. There's some palm trees, and below there's a dock where we
> have a little powered boat, and we watch the sunset from the deck.
> That is in some sense the statistical average of our dreams, and so I
> think that's really interesting that the more plastic we make [Second Life],
> the more it resembles whatever it is we want.

Of course, virtual decadence is not the only use of Second Life. For
example, Peter Yellowlees, a professor of clinical psychiatry at the
University of California, Davis, created a simulation in which Second
Life users could experience what it felt like to suffer from schizophrenia. But Rosedale's description does accurately capture the most
jarring aspect of Second Life as a whole: in a world where people can
become and create anything they want, the overwhelming desire is
to create a virtual Malibu on steroids. And this obsession with material decadence in a virtual world is probably the farthest you can be
from Barlow's "being in nothingness."[5]

As we saw in the chapter on superstitions, personal space matters
in cyberspace because we obey the rules we learn from the physical
world. This social training is what makes it psychologically awkward
to have a formal meeting with everyone standing even if our virtual
bodies don't get tired. We create virtual chairs because our physical
bodies get tired from standing. And once we have virtual furniture,
we need virtual room and houses to put all this furniture in. Instead
of escaping from physical reality, virtual worlds have become a way
for us to replicate physical reality.

In recent years, the commercial success and mainstream aware-
ness of virtual worlds, and online games in particular, have spurred a

broad interest in incorporating aspects of these virtual worlds into corporate work. One misconception I have repeatedly come across is that there is something magical about representing people and places in 3D—the notion that a virtual meeting room, classroom, or health fair is inherently engaging and fun. For nongamer businesspeople who see online games for the first time, the most immediate appeal is the 3D graphics. But the 3D is a red herring. After all, virtual chairs and virtual tables do not make work any more efficient or engaging. As we've seen, they may make things you take for granted in the physical world much more frustrating and time-consuming. And the first fundamental truth of virtual worlds is this: boring people are still boring when they are in 3D.

Three-dimensional avatars in online games have a hidden functionality that is not obvious to nongamers; they are actually designed to be inefficient. In golf, there is a reason why you're not allowed to pick up the ball and walk over to the hole. There would be no game of golf if rules did not explicitly constrain your ability to move the ball. Whether it's golf, Pac-Man, or chess, the obstruction creates the game. In *World of Warcraft*, players have to reach a certain level and accumulate a moderate amount of gold before they are able to purchase a mount that lets them move 60 percent faster. Characters have to manually walk to places to justify the mount being a reward. Forcing players to walk through a dungeon, instead of allowing them to teleport to a final battle at the boss chamber, is what creates danger and risk. The inefficiency is the game. In a virtual world designed for business interactions, this is the exact opposite of what users desire. You don't want workers to waste time walking to virtual places or putting virtual folders in virtual filing cabinets. Virtual worlds have rules that influence how we live and work in them. And when we do not explicitly question these rules, unintended consequences enslave us.

The fact that having a virtual body leads to liabilities instead of liberation was made clear even in early online textual worlds. The popularity of MUDs in the 1980s led Pavel Curtis, a researcher at Xerox PARC, to experiment with using these textual worlds for work-oriented contexts. Instead of having the geography and rules fully defined at the start, Curtis's variant allowed users to create their own content and modify the geography using a basic scripting language. There would be no overarching game rules or goals. Instead, users found a sandbox that they were free to expand as long as they followed basic ground rules. Curtis called these virtual worlds MOOs (MUD Object Oriented), and the first MOO, LambdaMOO, was created in the early 1990s. LambdaMOO was entirely textual. Users created descriptions for their characters, and other users could read these descriptions using the "look" command. Each room and every object in a room also had a textual description, again accessible with the "look" command. Other text commands allowed users to move around LambdaMOO and interact with other people and objects.[6]

The extensible sandbox nature of LambdaMOO allowed devious users to create scripts that subverted the ground rules. The Voodoo Doll is one such example. This script allowed a user to misattribute actions to other people as if they had typed out those actions themselves. Given that LambdaMOO was entirely textual, the Voodoo Doll, in effect, allowed a perpetrator to take control of another user's character. Julian Dibbell's 1993 article in the *Village Voice*, "A Rape in Cyberspace," famously captured one particularly gruesome use of the Voodoo Doll. A character named Mr._Bungle joined a crowd mingling in the living room and began using the Voodoo Doll on several people in the group: "As if against her will, Moondreamer jabs a steak knife up her ass, causing immense joy. You hear Mr._Bungle laughing evilly in the distance." These violent and sexual acts continued for hours as both victims and bystanders watched helplessly. This violation of virtual bodies led the administrators of LambdaMOO to create a user ballot and petition system to enable democratic self-governance. Although LambdaMOO remains active and is now more than twenty years old, it is telling that this malicious act against virtual bodies remains the best-known story from this virtual world. Our virtual bodies powerfully influence how we create and govern.[7]

Breaking the Rules

In *You Are Not a Gadget*, Jaron Lanier documents how technological decisions have a tendency to become entrenched and then, because of widespread dependencies, impossible to modify. A prime example is MIDI, a format created in the early 1980s to represent digital music. MIDI is behind almost all the music we hear around us—the synthetic beats and chords in popular music, cell phone ring tones and alarms, and so on—and has proven resistant to multiple attempts at reforming it in the ensuing decades. Lanier terms this process "lock-in": "Lock-in, however, removes design options based on what is easiest to program, what is politically feasible, what is fashionable, or what is created by chance."[8]

Lock-in puts up artificial blinders to how we see the world. The broad similarities in our contemporary virtual worlds and online games—users controlling one avatar in a geographical space that replicates physical navigation—distract us from the fact that we're locked in to one slice of a much larger possibility space. And the hype around virtual conference rooms misses a crucial point: Are we simply replicating physical chairs and tables in virtual worlds as a bloated alternative to teleconferencing by video? And although telecommunication is a worthwhile goal, we shouldn't allow it to subsume all other possibilities of virtual worlds. When we insist on replicating physical bodies and furniture, are we missing out on novel forms of work, collaboration, and play?

There is of course nothing wrong with having a digital body. After all, one good reason for relying on embodiment is that it provides a host of familiar and well-understood cues for social interaction—personal space, eye gaze, gestures, and so on. And familiar artifacts, such as virtual chairs and tables, create a well-understood context for social interactions. Thus, the chair at the head of the table has a social meaning that needs no elaborate explanation. And switching away from these familiar artifacts of embodiment might lead to confusion.

But it bears pointing out that the emergence of art, literacy, and science all hinged on finding alternative modes of representation. For example, music allows us to represent emotions, memories, and experiences in a novel way. Or, for example, our alphabet and writing system aren't based on the human body, but writing and poetry allow us to think, create, share, and interact in new ways. Moreover, even if we did accept the premise that familiar metaphors easily provide structure and meaning, there are still many other metaphors that we are familiar with apart from human bodies. Would a brainstorming meeting be more naturally structured using a representation revolving around a plant with its familiar concepts of offshoots, branches, maturity, incubation, and cross-pollination? At first glance, this seems more efficient than having virtual people putting up virtual Post-It notes on a virtual whiteboard. The virtual metaphor should change depending on the context and task.

A virtual world might also offer the possibility of serial embodiment. In this scenario, users have no default embodiment in the world but are free to take over or essentially possess other objects in the world, which grant them unique abilities. A person who likes to people-watch may possess a tree, blending into the environment but gaining heightened vision and hearing distances. Between embodiments, the user would be in ghost form. There is also no reason why we have to maintain a one-to-one relationship when it comes to virtual embodiment. Two or more users could possess the same object at the same time, with additional mechanics coming into play depending on whether they are able to collaborate with each other. In 2004, Blizzard announced a new playable race, the two-headed ogre, as an April Fool's joke. While this particular description of the race was impractical to play, a two- or multiplayer tandem control mechanic could conceivably lead to novel and interesting forms of play.

The repeated use of the same game formulas in online games has made it increasingly difficult to see other possibilities. As we read in the historical overview of online games, Raph Koster has stated that the implemented features of online games have actually shrunk rather than grown over time. In that same blog post, Koster noted that "the fact that people can cite things like 'big boss battles in a public zone' or 'really rich badge profiles and player stat tracking' as truly differentiating features mostly speaks to how narrow the scope of the field has gotten in the public's mind. This is like arguing over whether scalloped bracing in acoustic guitars is a defining characteristic for all of music." Thus, even though Blizzard's two-headed ogre idea was intended as a joke, the way it explicitly broke one of the core embodiment rules we've been locked into should have warranted more attention.[9]

In fact, imagining two heads is actually not that extreme, given that Lanier was experimenting with giving people eight arms in virtual reality in the 1980s. In these early explorations into putting people into virtual reality, graphical and code glitches were inevitable; sometimes digital bodies were warped or distorted. To Lanier's surprise, however, "It turned out that people could quickly learn to inhabit strange and different bodies and still interact with the virtual world. . . . I played around with elongated limb segments, and strange limb placement. The most curious experiment involved a virtual lobster." As with Barlow's initial reactions to cyberspace, Lanier is interested in using virtual reality to transcend the limits of how the physical human body experiences the world. In contrast, as we've seen throughout this chapter, most virtual worlds have been relegated to replicating the physical—bodies, clothes, houses, and furniture.[10]

The hidden logic in technology narrows the spectrum of possibilities into a small, comfortable bandwidth. We forget that the status quo is just one of many possible outcomes and often simply the arbitrary result of historical accidents. While we focus on the seemingly endless opportunities afforded by our virtual bodies, we shouldn't lose sight of the opportunities that our virtual bodies take away.

Current virtual worlds insist that each user has one avatar in the form of a human body and that these virtual bodies obey similar rules that govern the physical world—walking on two feet, not walking through walls, and so forth. As I've hinted at in this chapter, there are multiple ways to challenge this implicit orthodoxy. We could create virtual worlds in which users can control multiple avatars simultaneously, perhaps leaving avatars in automated idling behavior when switching among them. Instead of being virtual humans, I can imagine a virtual world in which players are different kinds of cells in a human body—the monsters are invading bacteria or viruses. Perhaps the virtual world is a rainforest ecosystem and players take on the role of different flora and fauna, trying to keep everything in balance. Or imagine a Benjamin Button world in which users start off in old avatars and get younger over time. What would it mean to raise a family and keep society running in such a world? I feel that virtual worlds offer us a chance to imagine the impossible, and we're all just a little too comfortable being in human bodies.

There is of course a middle ground. We could keep human bodies in virtual worlds of houses and furniture but tweak the rules of reality. Imagine a brainstorming room that facilitated turn-taking between participants. Perhaps the people who talk too much have progressively darker shadows, or they grow bigger and start to dwarf the others, or the people who are quiet start to fade away. To avoid agreement bias based on authority or gender, we might randomize the appearance of the other avatars for each participant. If we're stuck in virtual meeting rooms, we should at least take advantage of tools that would mitigate the inherent biases in group-based decision-making. I'm not suggesting that all these possibilities will be fruitful. But when we're given the chance to do and become anything we want, I feel we owe it to ourselves to try.

CHAPTER 12 REFLECTIONS AND THE FUTURE OF VIRTUAL WORLDS

In this book, I've focused on how online games often subvert the promises of freedom and escape. This is not to say that players never achieve transformative experiences. From the Daedalus Project surveys, two categories of players discuss finding escape and freedom in positive ways. The first group consists of those with physical disabilities.

> Several years ago, I was working as a nurse on the graveyard shift at a local hospital. While repositioning a patient, I seriously injured my back (L4−5 disk). I've been disabled and unable to work since then. MMORPGs have allowed me to interact with people and feel more whole/able. . . . With online gaming I can meet people and have something of a social life even while isolated and pretty debilitated in "real life." [*Star Wars Galaxies*, female, 46]

The second group comprises those who are struggling with issues of sexuality. Given the fear and uncertainty of coming out to friends and family, some players find a safe environment to explore and discuss their sexuality online.

> In my family guild there was a female character who was quite flirtatious, mostly with the guys but every once in a while with the

girls. . . . One day, after I mentioned having real-life ties to the gay community, this player confided in me that not only were they really male, but that they were a youngish gay male. He played a female to be able to flirt with the gender he preferred to flirt with. But, knowing the usual homophobia, he was careful to keep all relationships strictly on-line and banter. . . . I mentioned the GBLT guild on the other server to him and he cautiously made a female player there. Once he had a feel for the supportiveness of the GBLT guild, he promptly deleted the fe-male character and played an openly gay male character on that server in the GBLT guild. I think he said it was the first time he had played a male character without being in fear of saying the wrong thing to the wrong person. [City of Heroes, female, 40]

Responses like these, however, are uncommon in the Daedalus Proj-ect surveys as a whole. We have seen the social and psychological phenomena that have broad impact on virtual communities: how the operant conditioning that leads to superstitious behavior is some-thing we're all psychologically wired for, the way gold farming in online games has had a significant impact on the gaming landscape, and so forth. No doubt some players have found beneficial and trans-formative freedoms in online games, but I would argue that they are the exception.

There are three mutually nonexclusive trajectories that virtual worlds can take: they can replicate reality, influence reality, or re-imagine reality. Let me describe the possibilities of these different trajectories.

Replicating Reality

For all their dragons and magic, fantasy worlds actually aren't all that different from reality. One trajectory for virtual worlds is that they continue to perpetuate, reinforce, and produce social norms. Along with TV shows, movies, and magazines, virtual worlds become just another place where boys and girls learn what men and women are supposed to be. Virtual worlds create an appealing but illusory utopia, fooling us into thinking that ethnicity and global inequities no longer matter. They promise to transform us while preserving the status quo.

Oddly, the preservation of social norms has a silver lining. Social norms allow virtual worlds to be used to simulate and understand human behavior. The unintentional spread of a virulent in-game plague in *World of Warcraft* has prompted medical researchers to wonder if virtual worlds can be used to model and study epidemics. And Edward Castronova has argued that virtual worlds are "the modern equivalent to supercolliders for social scientists. . . . Virtual worlds allow for societal level research with no harm to humans, large numbers of experiments and participants, and make long term and panel studies possible." Indeed, the ability to collect longitudinal and detailed behavioral data from millions of people around the world has significant scientific potentials.[1]

Influencing Reality

Whether it's the avatar you're given, a doppelgänger of you, or the rules of the game, virtual worlds give us unparalleled tools for changing how we think and behave. Instead of providing an escape, virtual worlds can be used to influence how people behave offline. In this ironic trajectory, virtual worlds come to control reality. How we are influenced depends on the intentions of the manipulators. Virtual worlds may become a great way for retailers to make money from us. Our behavioral profiles in consuming entertainment reveal our material desires, allowing advertisers to target us more precisely. And for those who do not initially have such material desires, a doppelgänger might convince them that they need to buy something after all.

It is easy to underestimate the power of subtle manipulations because they are both so pervasive and so difficult to detect. But consider that the simple ordering of names on a presidential election ballot changes the vote outcome. In California's eighty assembly districts, the order of candidates on a ballot is randomly assigned. In 1994, Bill Clinton received 4 percent more votes in the districts in which he was listed first. In 2000, George W. Bush received 9 percent more votes when he was listed first. Even in high-profile elections in which voters presumably have thought about their preferences before arriving at the voting booth, the simple ordering of candidate names matters.[2]

This influence can be wielded for both good and bad. As we've seen, avatars can help people plan for their retirement. Ian Bogost, a game designer and media philosopher at the Georgia Institute of Technology, has used video games explicitly as social commentary. In one game that satirizes airport security procedures, players must quickly react to the capricious nature of the rules at the screening checkpoints. And game designer and researcher Jane McGonigal has created games that help people engage with pressing global issues, such as the reliance on fossil fuels. Unfortunately, the reality of our time is that major content creators need to care more about attracting large audiences than about generating highbrow social commentary. The programming shift on the History Channel, the Learning Channel, and the Discovery Channel—including attempts to gain broader market share via sensationalist coverage of aliens, a family with nineteen kids, and child pageants—stems from this market dynamic. And

I have a hard time believing that advertisers will care more about social well-being than their bottom line.

Reimagining Reality

Virtual worlds hold infinite possibilities, but so far we've explored only a sliver of those potentials. Yet we've seen that sliver replicated and superficially modified so often that it's easy to convince ourselves that we've covered a great deal of ground. Instead of replicating reality, virtual worlds could allow us to imagine new ones. Early textual virtual worlds allowed users to invent their own gender, but contemporary virtual worlds often provide just two options. Would leaving our bodies behind or creating novel forms of embodiment allow us to imagine new forms of work, play, and interaction? This issue is particularly relevant for business applications. Avatars don't inherently make work more efficient or more fun, but they certainly make people more distracted by their virtual hair and clothes. Certainly, some of the alternatives I've mentioned in the previous chapter may seem impractical, but I didn't think that the goal of virtual worlds was to be practical.

Sadly, it's not clear that we would embrace this freedom even if it were handed to us. We gravitate toward the familiar; bodies in virtual worlds may function as McDonald's does when we're looking for food in foreign countries. They are a necessary psychological anchor in a sea of uncertainty. And perhaps we replicate the darker parts of our offline lives in virtual worlds—work, stereotypes, and conflict— because they are nevertheless comforting and help moor us to the only reality we know. Research in early textual virtual worlds highlights this resistance to change. In these worlds, users were not constrained by graphical representations; avatars were created via textual descriptions alone. And yet, users often created avatars that leveraged racial tropes and stereotypes. As digital media researcher Lisa Nakamura has documented, many Asian-appearing avatars in Lambda-MOO borrowed heavily from martial arts or samurai movies. Perhaps the hypermaterialism of *Second Life* isn't caused by the presence of avatars. Perhaps it's just human nature.[3]

How Do We Get There?

These three trajectories are all somewhat double-edged, but even if it were clear that we need to try harder to use virtual worlds to re-imagine reality, I'm not sure gamers or laypeople could do much to influence the shift. This is primarily due to the significant costs in creating and maintaining virtual worlds. *World of War*craft took over $60 million to create, and that doesn't take into account the continuous operating costs. Only large corporations and game developers have the capital to create virtual worlds. Not only does this limit the ability of laypeople and even academic researchers to create their own virtual worlds, but it restricts the kinds of online games created due to risk adversity (and understandably so, given the entry fee).

Of course, there is also funding for virtual worlds from federal agencies, but here, too, the tendency is to create virtual worlds that replicate reality with ever higher fidelity. In the previous chapter, I mentioned the cross-cultural military training simulation developed by the Institute of Creative Technologies. That effort was made possible by a $45 million grant from the US Army. The institute collaborates with film studios and video game designers with the understanding that any new techniques developed are free to be used in video games and movies. There are also similar virtual simulations for training in other areas and to help soldiers overcome post-traumatic stress disorder. Replicating reality is a key goal of the military's interest in virtual worlds because the training context needs to match the actual context, and this has a trickle-down effect in terms of the technologies and graphical assets that are then available for commercial use.[4]

And there's the rub. Experimentation in virtual worlds is expensive and resource-intensive, requiring very specialized skills in 3D graphics, server optimization, game design, storytelling, community management, and so forth. It's difficult for gamers or even tech-savvy folks to put together a prototype. But we have seen the democratization of technology occur in other areas. Blogging software gave everyone the ability to create their own website without needing to learn a single HTML tag. And Picasa allowed everyone to manage, edit, and share their digital photos without needing to learn a complex photo-editing package or understand photography concepts such as white balance. Raph Koster, lead designer of *Ultima Online* and *Star Wars Galaxies*, began development of a software platform called Metaplace that would have allowed anyone to create his or her own virtual world with a low barrier of entry. If you wanted a kingdom of fluffy cloud animals, you could build that. If you wanted a storytelling game set at Downton Abbey, you could build that, too. Unfortunately, the Metaplace platform closed in 2010, but I strongly believe that we need something like Metaplace to move us along our experimentation with virtual worlds. Since the boom days of *World of Warcraft* and *Second Life*, there has been a strange, stagnant lull in terms of virtual worlds. I think gamers and academics have kept wondering what would come next in either the online gaming or social virtual worlds spaces, but nothing has transpired to shift the attention from these two existing worlds. Yet in the same way that blogging software has allowed everyone to become comfortable with digital publishing and sharing (which helped to pave the way for social networking sites), it is only by lowering the entry cost of virtual world creation that we can understand the full potential of virtual worlds. Instead of being content to visit virtual worlds, we need to ask ourselves what new worlds we would create if we had the chance.

NOTES

Introduction

1. Homer *Odyssey* 4.446–448, trans. Richmond Lattimore (New York: Harper Perennial, 2007), 77.

2. To avoid these unwieldy labels, I refer to games in this genre as simply "online games" in this book. "12 million" reported in Blizzard press release; see http://us.blizzard.com/en-us/company/press/pressreleases.html?id=2847881. Estimates of active online gaming subscriptions and peak concurrent usage come from MMO-Data.net, v. 3.8, retrieved on January 10, 2012. For online games forecast in China, see John Gaudiosi, "Booming Chinese MMO Games Market Forecast to Generate $6.1 Billion in 2012," *Forbes*, June 6, 2012. For statistics of Club Penguin, see Brooks Barnes, "Disney Acquires Web Site for Children," *New York Times*, August 2, 2007. It is difficult to get an accurate estimate of worldwide MMO gamers because subscription numbers are often closely guarded by game companies, different metrics are used for free-to-play games than for subscription-based games, and marketing companies count different kinds of games as "online games"—for example, some reports will include nonpersistent games (such as *World of Tanks* or *League of Legends*) as an MMO. The boom of casual web and smart phone games that are played online confuses these estimates even more.

3. Olga Kazan, "Lost in an Online Fantasy World," *Washington Post*, August 18, 2006; Vicki Haddock, "Online Danger Zone," *San Francisco Chronicle*, February 12, 2006; Edward Castronova, *Synthetic Worlds: The Business and Culture of Online Games* (Chicago: University of Chicago Press, 2005), 76.

4. Sherry Turkle, *Life on the Screen* (New York: Touchstone, 1997), 263–264; Bonnie A. Nardi, *My Life as a Night Elf Priest: An Anthropological Account of World of Warcraft* (Ann Arbor: University of Michigan Press, 2010), 7.

5. A more detailed methodology description of the Daedalus Project can be found in Nick Yee, "The Demographics, Motivations and Derived Experiences of Users of Massively-Multiuser Online Graphical Environments," *Presence* 15 (2006): 309–329.

Chapter One. The New World

1. *Kriegsspiel* is described in Tim Lenoir and Henry Lowood, "Theatres of War: The Military-Entertainment Complex," in *Kunstkammer, Laboratorium, Bühne—Schauplätze des Wissens im 17. Jahrhundert*, ed. Jan Lazardig, Helmar Schramm, and Ludger Scharte (Berlin: Walter de Gruyter, 2003). The full text of H. G. Wells's *Little Wars* is available at Project Gutenberg: http://www.gutenberg.org/ebooks/3691.

2. Scott Lynch, "Industry Insights: The RPGNet Interviews: Interview with Gary Gygax," *RPGNet* (2001), available at: http://www.rpg.net/news+reviews/columns/lynch01may01.html.

3. Interview with TheOneRing.net, available at: http://archives.theonering.net/features/interviews/gary_gygax.html. See also Gygax's interview with Game Spy in 2004, available at: http://pc.gamespy.com/articles/538/538817p3.html.

4. For the history of the PLATO system, see Stanley G. Smith and Bruce Arne Sherwood, "Educational Uses of the PLATO Computer System," *Science* 23 (1976): 344–352. For the history of *Maze War*, see Anthony Steed and Manuel Fradinho Oliveira, *Networked Graphics: Building Networked Games and Virtual Environments* (Burlington, MA: Morgan Kaufmann, 2010), 23.

5. Dennis G. Jerz, "Somewhere Nearby Is Colossal Cave: Examining Will Crowther's Original 'Adventure' in Code and Kentucky," *Digital Humanities Quarterly* 1, no. 2 (2007), available at: http://www.digitalhumanities.org/dhq/vol/001/2/000009/000009.html.

6. Richard Bartle, "Early MUD History," available at: http://www.mud.co.uk/richard/mudhist.htm. See also Richard Bartle, *Designing Virtual Worlds* (Indianapolis, IN: New Riders, 2004), 4–7. For ARPANet and MUD, see Koster's timeline of virtual worlds in Jessica Mulligan and Bridgette Patrovsky, *Developing Online Games: An Insider's Guide* (Indianapolis, IN: New Riders, 2003), also available online at: http://www.raphkoster.com/gaming/mudtimeline.shtml.

7. See Koster's timeline.

8. See Damion Schubert's postmortem of *Meridian 59* in Mulligan and Patrovsky, *Developing Online Games*.

9. Subscriber estimates of *EverQuest* and *Ultima Online* are drawn from MMOData.net, specifically the historical charts for 150,000 to 1 million subscribers. See also Bartle, *Designing Virtual Worlds*, 20–29, on how *Ultima Online* and *EverQuest* changed the field.

10. Subscription numbers of *World of Warcraft* drawn from MMOData.net. The original Blizzard press release announcing breaking the one million subscriber mark

in Europe was posted on January 19, 2006, but is no longer available on Blizzard's website. A copy of the press release is available at: http://www.mmorpg.com/gamelist.cfm/setView /news/gameID/15/showArticle/4427.

11. As Bartle explains, "mobile" originally referred, not to movement per se, but to the moving sculptures, "because creatures moving in a controlled but unpredictable way are like the kind of 'mobiles' that hang from the ceiling" (*Designing Virtual Worlds*, 102).

12."Nothing to do": ibid., 5. In Hans-Henrik Starfeldt's original 1990 alt.mud post calling for developers on his new MUD, he wrote that "we think the preatent [sic] games has lost some of the D&D spirit (with all respect!)." Koster's "Simultaneously and independently" and "removed more features": Koster blog post on MUD influence on online games: http://www.raphkoster.com/2008/06/27/mud-influence/. Bartle's "grew in a particular way": Metanomics interview in *Second Life*: http://www.metanomics.net/show/archive031008/.

13. The first game in the city-building genre to introduce a limited multiplayer mode was Sierra's *Emperor: Rise of the Middle Kingdom* in 2002. Monte Cristo's *Cities XL* had a massively multiplayer mode when it launched in 2009, but Monte Cristo closed this multiplayer option after five months. I consider the shallow and asynchronous multiplayer options in city-building games on Facebook and mobile devices to be different beasts altogether.

Chapter Two. **Who Plays and Why**

1. For a historical perspective on gaming, see Dmitri Williams, "A Brief Social History of Video Games," in *Playing Computer Games: Motives, Responses, and Consequences*, ed. Peter Vorderer and Jennings Bryant (Mahwah, NJ: Lawrence Erlbaum, 2006), 229–247. For Williams's news media analysis, see Dmitri Williams, "The Video Game Lightning Rod: Constructions of a New Media Technology," *Information, Communication and Society* 6 (2003): 523–550.

2. For recurrence of moral panics, see Ellen Wartella and Byron Reeves, "Historical Trends in Research on Children and the Media: 1900–1960," *Journal of Communication* 35 (2006): 118–133. For historical overview of the comic book moral panic, see James Gilbert, *A Cycle of Outrage: America's Reaction to the Juvenile Delinquent in the 1950s* (New York: Oxford University Press, 1988). Angela McRobbie, "The Moral Panic in the Age of the Postmodern Mass Media," in *Postmodernism and Popular Culture* (London: Routledge, 1994), 192–213.

3. Jimmy Kimmel interview with Mila Kunis, *Jimmy Kimmel Live!* October 17, 2008.

4. For studies that provide demographic data on online gamers over the past decade, see Mark D. Griffiths, Mark N. O. Davies, and Darren Chappell, "Breaking the Stereotype: The Case of Online Gaming," *CyberPsychology and Behavior* 6 (2003): 81–91; Nick Yee, "The Demographics, Motivations, and Derived Experiences of Users of

Massively Multi-User Online Graphical Environments," *Presence: Teleoperators and Virtual Environments* 15 (2006): 309–329; Dmitri Williams, Nick Yee, and Scott E. Caplan, "Who Plays, How Much, and Why? Debunking the Stereotypical Gamer Profile," *Journal of Computer-Mediated Communication* 13 (2008): 993–1018; and Nick Yee, Nicolas Ducheneaut, Mike Yao, and Les Nelson, "Do Men Heal More When in Drag? Conflicting Identity Cues between User and Avatar," *Proceedings of CHI 2011* (2011): 773–776. For estimates of online gamers who are teenagers, Griffiths, Davies, and Chappel, "Breaking the Stereotype," found 40%; Yee, "Demographics, Motivations, and Derived Experiences," found 25%; and Williams, Yee, and Caplan, "Who Plays," found roughly 10%. The average of these numbers is 25%.

5. On the percentage of female players, Williams, Yee, and Caplan, "Who Plays," report 19.2%, and Yee, "Demographics, Motivations, and Derived Experiences," reports 15%. In a Daedalus Project sample of 1,109 *World of Warcraft* players in 2005, I found 16%, but in a more recent study of *World of Warcraft* gamers reported in 2011, my colleagues and I found 26%; Nick Yee, Nicolas Ducheneaut, Les Nelson, and Peter Likarish, "Introverted Elves and Conscientious Gnomes: The Expression of Personality in World of Warcraft," *Proceedings of CHI 2011* (2011): 753–762. The 20% reported in the text is a rough average of these figures. Younger players are more likely to enjoy leadership positions in online games. Whereas younger players are more likely to start a guild, older players tend to assume the leadership role at some point down the line. See Nick Yee, "Being a Leader," *The Daedalus Project* (2005): http://www.nickyee.com/daedalus/archives/001467.php; and Nick Yee, "The Origin of Guild Leaders," *The Daedalus Project* (2006): http://www.nickyee.com/daedalus/archives/001517.php.

6. Part of this cross-cultural data has been reported in papers focusing on different aspects of gameplay. See, e.g., Nick Yee, Nicolas Ducheneaut, and Les Nelson, "Online Gaming Motivations Scale: Development and Validation," *Proceedings of CHI 2012* (2012): 2803–2806. But the full cross-cultural data from the entire study have never been reported, so I mention the new data here: the average age of online gamers in the United States was 34.2 (SD = 10.7, n = 876); in the European Union, 32.6 (SD = 8.6, n = 279); and in mainland China, 22.3 (SD = 3.6, n = 640). Owing to institutional review board restrictions at the federal research level, we were unable to collect data from minors, so these data points are skewed higher than the true averages.

7. In terms of average hours of play each week, Yee, "Demographics, Motivations, and Derived Experiences," reported a mean of 22.7 hours and a median of 20 hours per week. Williams, Yee, and Caplan, "Who Plays," reported a mean of 25.7 hours per week. Yee found no significant correlation between age and hours played; Williams, Yee, and Caplan found a significant positive correlation. For average TV watching in the United States, see Nielsen, "Report: How Americans Are Spending Their Media Time . . . and Money," www.nielsenwire.com, February 9, 2012, available at:

http://blog.nielsen.com/nielsenwire/online_mobile/report-how-americans-are-spending-their-media-time-and-money/.

8. Frequency of playing together with people outside the game has been reported in multiple papers, but often grouped in different ways. In Yee, "Demographics, Motivations, and Derived Experiences," 16% of male players and 60% of female players regularly played with a romantic partner; 26% of male players and 40% of female players did so with family members. In Helena Cole and Mark D. Griffiths, "Social Interactions in Massively Multiplayer Online Role-Playing Games," *CyberPsychology and Behavior* 10 (2007): 575–583, 26% played with family and friends. The data reported in the text come from Nick Yee, "Playing with Someone," *The Daedalus Project* (2005): available at http://www.nickyee.com/daedalus/archives/001468.php, which lists the percentages by category and then the summed overlap across the categories.

9. Positive and negative experiences data points are drawn from Yee, "Demographics, Motivations, and Derived Experiences," as is the friendship comparability issue. Cole and Griffiths, "Social Interactions in Massively Multiplayer Online Role-Playing Games," report a similar finding on friendship comparability, 46%.

10. For Bartle's player types, see Richard Bartle, "Hearts, Clubs, Diamonds, Spades: Players Who Suit MUDS" (1996), available at: http://www.mud.co.uk/richard/hcds.htm. Factor analysis was used to identify these motivation clusters. See Nick Yee, "Motivations for Play in Online Games," *CyberPsychology and Behavior* 9 (2006): 772–775; and the validation of the scale in Nick Yee, Nicolas Ducheneaut, and Les Nelson, "Online Gaming Motivations Scale: Development and Validation," *Proceedings of CHI 2012* (2012): 2803–2806.

11. The research in problematic Internet usage has tended to dovetail with research in problematic gaming, suggesting that both depression and social anxiety are significant contributors. See Marcantonio M. Spada, Benjamin Langston, Ana V. Nikčević, and Giovanni B. Moneta, "The Role of Metacognitions in Problematic Internet Usage," *Computers in Human Behavior* 24 (2008): 2325–2335; Robert LaRose, Carolyn A. Lin, and Matthew S. Eastin, "Unregulated Internet Usage: Addiction, Habit, or Deficient Self-Regulation?" *Media Psychology* 5 (2003): 225–253; and Scott E. Caplan, Dmitri Williams, and Nick Yee, "Problematic Internet Use and Psychosocial Well-Being among MMO Players," *Computers in Human Behavior* 25 (2009): 1312–1319. For the study on family members playing together, see Cuihua Shen and Dmitri Williams, "Unpacking Time Online: Connecting Internet and MMO Use with Psychosocial Well-Being," *Communication Research* 38 (2011): 123–149.

12. Andrew J. Grundstein et al., "A Retrospective Analysis of American Football Hyperthermia Deaths in the United States," *International Journal of Biometeorology* 56 (2010): 11.

Chapter Three. **Superstitions**

1. B. F. Skinner, *The Behavior of Organisms* (New York: Appleton-Century-Crofts, 1938).

2. B. F. Skinner, "'Superstition' in the Pigeon," *Journal of Experimental Psychology* 38 (1948): 168–172.

3. Alfred Bruner and Samuel H. Revusky, "Collateral Behavior in Humans," *Journal of the Experimental Analysis of Behavior* 4 (1961): 349–350.

4. Heather Sinclair discusses some of these superstitions in a comment to a blog post on Terra Nova: http://terranova.blogs.com/terra_nova/2006/10/superstition.html#c25369047.

5. Byron Reeves and Clifford Nass, *The Media Equation: How People Treat Computers, Televisions, and New Media Like Real People and Places* (New York: Cambridge University Press, 1996).

6. See Michael Argyle and Janet Dean, "Eye-Contact, Distance and Affiliation," *Sociometry* 28 (1965): 289–304; and Nick Yee et al., "The Unbearable Likeness of Being Digital: The Persistence of Nonverbal Social Norms in Online Virtual Environments," *Journal of CyberPsychology and Behavior* 10 (2007): 115–121.

7. There are many other examples of these cognitive shortcuts. See, e.g., Amos Tversky and Daniel Kahneman, "Judgment under Uncertainty: Heuristics and Biases," *Science* 185 (1974): 1124–1131.

8. For examples of known effects of moon phases in *Final Fantasy XI*, see this wiki page: http://wiki.ffxiclopedia.org/wiki/Moon_Phase. Note how the unproven effects of moon phases are explicitly marked.

9. The player behind Wi describes the early dismissal of his digital torment on this guild post: http://www.gamerdna.com/GuildHome.php?guildid=5849&page=2. Turbine's initial denial and subsequent discovery of the bug were originally released at: http://www.zone.com/asheronscall/news/ASHEletter0702.asp. That link is no longer available, but the letter has been archived and is available at: http://asheron.wikia.com/wiki/Wi_Flag.

Chapter Four. **The Labor of Fun**

1. In game studies, the philosophical distinction between play and nonplay usually centers on debates around the concept of the "magic circle"—the special space created by a game that marks it off from reality—originally coined by Johan Huizinga in *Homo Ludens: A Study of Play Element in Culture* (Boston: Beacon, 1938). It is a highly abstract and theoretical discussion, and I refer interested readers to a recent review of the literature: Jaakko Stenros, "In Defence of a Magic Circle: The Social and Mental Boundaries of Play," *Proceedings of 2012 DiGRA Nordic* (2012), http://www.digra.org/dl/db/12168.43543.pdf. See also Bonnie A. Nardi, "Work, Play, and the Magic

Circle," in *My Life as a Night Elf Priest: An Anthropological Account of World of Warcraft* (Ann Arbor: University of Michigan Press, 2010), 94–122.

2. One of many equations from the "SWG Profession Guide—Doctor": http://forum.galaxiesreborn.com/star-wars-galaxies-profession-guides/swg-profession-guide-doctor-t3208.html.

3. Excerpted from: www.hadean.org in 2005.

4. Excerpted from: http://eve-search.com/thread/622081/page/1.

5. Full interview available at: http://www.nickyee.com/daedalus/archives/001334.php.

6. Here, "classism" refers to the periodic preferences and non-preferences for certain classes in the game owing to changes in game balancing. Classes that are perceived as nonoptimal may be shunned by other players when forming raids and dungeon groups.

7. John C. Beck and Mitchell Wade, *Got Game: How the Gamer Generation Is Reshaping Business Forever* (Boston: Harvard Business School, 2004).

8. Jane McGonigal, *Reality Is Broken: Why Games Make Us Better and How They Can Change the World* (New York: Penguin, 2011); Byron Reeves and J. Leighton Read, *Total Engagement: Using Games and Virtual Worlds to Change the Way People Work and Businesses Compete* (Boston: Harvard Business School, 2009).

9. "Gartner Says by 2014, 80 Percent of Current Gamified Applications Will Fail to Meet Business Objectives Primarily Due to Poor Design," *Gartner Newsroom*, November 27, 2012, www.gartner.com/newsroom/id/2251015.

10. See Tiziana Terranova, "Free Labor: Producing Culture for the Digital Economy," *Social Text* 63 (2000): 33–58. For more on free labor, see Trebor Scholz, ed., *Internet as Playground and Factory* (New York: Routledge, 2012). For news coverage of the protein folding game, see Michael J. Coren and Fast Company, "Foldit Gamers Solve Riddle of HIV Enzyme within 3 Weeks," *Scientific American*, September 20, 2011. For more on how gamification can be exploitative, see Ian Bogost, "Persuasive Games: Exploitationware," *Gamasutra*, May 3, 2011, available at: http://www .gamasutra.com /view/feature/6366/persuasive_games_exploitation ware.php.

Chapter Five. **Yi-Shan-Guan**

1. These player-made videos first reported in Constance Steinkuehler, "The Mangle of Play," *Games and Culture* 1 (2006): 199–213.

2. Nicolas Ducheneaut, Nick Yee, Eric Nickell, and Robert J. Moore, "Building an MMO with Mass Appeal: A Look at Gameplay in World of Warcraft," *Games and Culture* 1 (2006): 281–317.

3. Julian Dibbell, "The Life of a Chinese Gold Farmer," *New York Times*, June 17, 2007.

4. Richard Heeks, "Current Analysis and Future Research Agenda on 'Gold

Farming': Real-World Production in Developing Countries for Virtual Economies of Online Games," *Development Informatics Working Paper Series* (2008), retrieved from: http://www.sed.manchester.ac.uk/idpm/research/publications/wp/di/di_wp32.htm.

5. Danny Vincent, "China Used Prisoners in Lucrative Internet Gaming Work," *Guardian*, May 25, 2011.

6. In games like *World of Warcraft*, PvP on most servers is meant to be a mutually consensual activity. Players can toggle their PvP status. When toggled off, no other player can attack them. When toggled on, they can attack other PvP-flagged players. If a non-PvP-flagged Player A attacks a PvP-flagged Player B, Player A's PvP-flag is toggled on. Gold farmers sometimes try to trick normal players by first toggling on their PvP-flag and then step into monsters the player is attacking, hoping that the player clicks on them instead of the monster and accidentally causing them to become PvP-flagged. When this happens, the gold farmer can attack and attempt to kill the player via PvP. In resource-rich areas, there are often multiple gold farmers. Thus, when normal players are tricked to becoming PvP-flagged, they may be set upon by multiple gold farmers.

7. Heeks, "Current Analysis and Future Research Agenda," 11–12.

8. Thread now defunct but originally available at: http://forums.worldofwar craft.com/thread.aspx?FN=wow-mage&T=283346.

9. Thread now defunct but originally available at: http://forums.worldofwar craft.com/thread.aspx?FN=wow-general&T=4007590.

10. Lisa Nakamura, "Don't Hate the Player, Hate the Game: The Racialization of Labor in World of Warcraft," *Critical Studies in Media Communication* 26 (2009): 128–144.

11. Dean Chan, "Being Played: Games Culture and Asian American Dis/Identifications," *Refractory* 16 (2009): 1.

12. See http://web.archive.org/web/20060708212246/http://www.hellomon ster.net/2006/04/18/blizzards-patriot-act/.

13. *Yi-shan-guan* was a euphemism that implied a tailoring or clothing emporium, without any direct reference to washing or laundry. Iris Chang, *The Chinese in America: A Narrative History* (New York: Penguin Books, 2003), 48–49, 169.

14. Ibid., 119, 132.

15. Edward Castronova, "Is Inflation Fun?" *Terra Nova*, http://terranova.blogs.com /terra_nova/2005/08/is_inflation_fu.html.

16. Heeks, "Current Analysis and Future Research Agenda," 23.

17. Nate Combs, "Why Are In-Game Economies so Hard to Get Right?" *TerraNova*, http://terranova.blogs.com/terra_nova/2004/02/why_are_ingame_.html.

18. This finding on lynching was first reported in C. Hovland and R. Sears, "Minor Studies of Aggression: Correlation of Lynchings with Economic Indices," *Journal of Psychology: Interdisciplinary and Applied* 9 (1940): 301–310. A reanalysis revealed some statistical flaws, but the corrected analysis still showed the same correlations at a lower magnitude: Alexander Mintz, "A Re-Examination of Correlations between

Lynchings and Economic Indices," *Journal of Abnormal Social Psychology* 41 (1946): 154–160. A definitive reanalysis using time series analysis has confirmed that the correlations are real and not simply artifacts of incorrect statistics: E. M. Beck and Stewart E. Tolnay, "The Killing Fields of the Deep South: The Market for Cotton and the Lynchings of Blacks," *American Sociological Review* 55 (1990): 526–539. The study of ethnic stereotypes in the European Union is reported in Edwin Poppe, "Effects of Changes in GNP and Perceived Group Characteristics on National and Ethnic Stereotypes in Central and Eastern Europe," *Journal of Applied Social Psychology* 31 (2006): 1689–1708.

Chapter Six. **The Locker Room Utopia**

1. Edward Castronova, *Synthetic Worlds: The Business and Culture of Online Games* (Chicago: University of Chicago Press, 2005). Statistics of gender ratio across all video games can be found in Entertainment Software Association, "2012 Essential Facts about the Computer and Video Game Industry," http://www.theesa.com/facts/pdfs/ESA_EF_2012.pdf. The ratio of female gamers is reported as 26% in a study of *World of Warcraft* players in Nick Yee, Nicolas Ducheneaut, Han-Tai Shiao, and Les Nelson, "Through the Azerothian Looking Glass: Mapping In-Game Preferences to Real World Demographics," *Proceedings of CHI 2012* 1 (2012): 2811–2814; as 19.7% women in a study of *EverQuest II* players in Dmitri Williams, Mia Consalvo, Scott Caplan, and Nick Yee, "Looking for Gender: Gender Roles and Behaviors among Online Gamers," *Journal of Communication* 59 (2009): 700–725; and as 15% women in an earlier study across multiple online games in Nick Yee, "The Demographics, Motivations, and Derived Experiences of Users of Massively Multi-User Online Graphical Environments," *Presence* 15 (2006): 309–329.

2. Torben Grodal, "Video Games and the Pleasure of Control," in *Media Entertainment: The Psychology of Its Appeal*, ed. Dolf Zillman and Peter Vorderer (Mahwah, NJ: Lawrence Erlbaum, 2000), 197–213; Kristen Lucas and John L. Sherry, "Sex Differences in Video Game Play: A Communication-Based Explanation," *Communication Research* 31 (2004): 499–523; Chris Crawford, "Women in Games," *Escapist* 17 (2005): 3–9.

3. T. L. Taylor, *Play between Worlds: Exploring Online Game Culture* (Cambridge, MA: MIT Press, 2006), 113.

4. Holin Lin, "Body, Space, and Gendered Gaming Experiences: A Cultural Geography of Homes, Cybercafés and Dormitories," *Beyond Barbie and Mortal Kombat: New Perspectives on Gender and Computer Games*, ed. Yasmin B. Kafai et al. (Cambridge, MA: MIT Press, 2008), 54–67.

5. Parenting differences in arcade access reported in Desmond Ellis, "Video Arcades, Youth, and Trouble," *Youth and Society* 16 (1984): 47–65. For Williams's studies of women in gaming, see Dmitri Williams, Nicole Martins, Mia Consalvo, and James D. Ivory, "The Virtual Census: Representations of Gender, Race and Age in

Video Games," *New Media and Society* 11 (2009): 815–834; and Dmitri Williams, "A Brief Social History of Video Games," in *Playing Computer Games: Motives, Responses, and Consequences*, ed. Peter Vorderer and Jennings Bryant (Mahwah, NJ: Lawrence Erlbaum, 2006), 229–247.

6. David Alan Grier, *When Computers Were Human* (Princeton, NJ: Princeton University Press, 2005); T. Camp, "Women in Computer Studies: Reversing the Trend," *Syllabus* 24 (2001): 24–26; Computing Research Association, "Computing Degree and Enrollment Trends," http://www .cra.org/uploads/documents/resources/taulbee/CS_Degree _and_Enrollment_Trends_2010–11.pdf.

7. Yee, "Demographics, Motivations and Derived Experiences."

8. Jennifer Jenson and Suzanne de Castell, "Her Own Boss: Gender and the Pursuit of Incompetent Play" (Paper presented at DiGRA 2005).

9. In the interest of full disclosure, I am currently employed by Ubisoft, but since I had previously recounted this story with Romine in a book chapter long before I was employed by Ubisoft, I felt it was acceptable to reproduce it here without seeming too biased.

10. See http://www.nickyee.com/daedalus/archives/001557.php.

11. Sheri Graner Ray, *Gender Inclusive Game Design: Expanding the Market* (Hingham, MA: Charles River Media, 2004), 104.

12. http://us.battle.net/d3/en/forum/topic/5968887243.

13. Here are three studies that report very consistent gender differences in gaming: T. Hartmann and C. Klimmt, "Gender and Computer Games: Exploring Females' Dislikes," *Journal of Computer-Mediated Communication* 11 (2006): 910–931; Lucas and Sherry, "Sex Differences in Video Game Play"; and Williams, Consalvo, Caplan, and Yee, "Looking for Gender." In addition to the last source cited, I've also reported this in a different data set: Nick Yee, "Motivations for Play in Online Games," *Journal of CyberPsychology and Behavior* 9 (2006): 772–775.

14. Nick Yee, "WoW Alliance vs. Horde," *The Daedalus Project*, available at: http://www.nickyee.com/daedalus/archives/001366.php.

15. The overlap percentage U between two samples can be calculated based on the effect size d, as described in: J. Cohen, *Statistical Power Analysis for the Behavioral Sciences* (Mahwah, NH: Lawrence Erlbaum, 1988). For the data here, I used the effect sizes from the data in Yee, "Motivations for Play in Online Games." The effect size for the Mechanics motivation was $r = .24$. The average effect size across all 10 motivations was $r = .12$. These convert to effect size d as .49 and .25, respectively. The distribution overlap percentages were then estimated based on these effect size metrics. For the data from Williams, see Consalvo, Caplan, and Yee, "Looking for Gender." The effect size d can be calculated based on the means and standard deviations reported in table 1, resulting in d = .44. Hyde's argument can be found in Janet Shibley Hyde, "The Gender Similarities Hypothesis," *American Psychologist* 60 (2005): 581–592.

16. This analysis uses data reported in Yee, "Demographics, Motivations and

Derived Experiences." Variance explained can be estimated by squaring the effect size metric r. The effect size r for gender in the Achievement motivation is .26, while effect size for age is .33. The resulting variances explained are .07 and .11, respectively.

17. This phenomenon is incredibly consistent across time and games. For early data from *EverQuest* players, see http://nickyee.com/eqt/genderbend.html. For recent data from *World of Warcraft* players, see Nick Yee, Nicolas Ducheneaut, Mike Yao, and Les Nelson, "Do Men Heal More When in Drag? Conflicting Identity Cues between User and Avatar," *Proceedings of CHI 2012 I* (2012): 773–776. This phenomenon was also reported in early text-based virtual worlds: Amy S. Bruckman, "Gender Swapping on the Internet," *Proceedings of INET* (Reston, VA: Internet Society, 1993). For the post on the Daedalus Project, see: http://www.nickyee.com/daedalus/archives/001369.php. When the gender disparity of gender-bending is brought up, it is often framed from the male perspective: Why do men gender-bend so much? This perspective assumes that veridicality is the norm and that men are somehow breaking this norm. It bears pointing out that this may be the less fruitful of the two options. From a feminist perspective, there would, on the surface, seem to be good reasons for women to gender-bend—to reject the objectification of female bodies. On the other hand, the need to reject your own biological sex to feel comfortable in a social space highlights a core problem in these online games for women. In either case, the question we should be asking might be: Why is gender-bending among women so uncommon in online games?

18. Nick Yee, Nicolas Ducheneaut, Les Nelson, and Peter Likarish, "Introverted Elves and Conscientious Gnomes: The Expression of Personality in World of Warcraft," *Proceedings of CHI 2011* (2011): 753–762.

19. Jesse Fox and Jeremy N. Bailenson, "Virtual Virgins and Vamps: The Effects of Exposure to Female Characters' Sexualized Appearance and Gaze in an Immersive Virtual Environment," *Sex Roles* 61 (2009): 147–157.

20. Langdon Winner, *The Whale and the Reactor: A Search for Limits in an Age of High Technology* (Chicago: University of Chicago Press, 1998), 21–22.

21. See Marybeth J. Mattingly and Suzanne M. Bianchi, "Gender Differences in Quantity and Quality of Free Time: The U.S. Experience," *Social Forces* 81 (2003): 999–1030; and Lyn Craig and Killian Mullan, "Parental Leisure Time: A Gender Comparison in Five Countries," *Social Politics* (2013), doi: 10.1093/sp/jxt002. For examples of how guilt is used in advertising directed at women, see Katherine J. Parkin, *Food Is Love: Advertising and Gender Roles in Modern America* (Philadelphia: University of Pennsylvania Press, 2006).

22. The anecdote from the Difference Engine Initiative reported in Stephanie Fisher and Alison Harvey, "Intervention for Inclusivity: Gender Politics and Indie Game Development," *Loading . . . Journal of the Canadian Game Studies Association* 7 (2013): 25–40. Gabrielle Toledano, "Women and Video Gaming's Dirty Little Secrets," *Forbes,*

January 18, 2013, http://www.forbes.com/sites/forbeswomanfiles/2013/01/18
/women-and-video-gamings-dirty-little-secrets/

Chapter Seven. The "Impossible" Romance

1. Lindsy Van Gelder, "Strange Case of the Electronic Lover," *Ms.* 14 (1985): 94, 99, 101–104, 117, 123, 124.

2. T. L. Taylor, *Play between Worlds: Exploring Online Game Culture* (Cambridge, MA: MIT Press, 2006), 52. Pew Internet survey results from M. Madden and A. Lenhart, "Online Dating," *Pew Internet and American Life Project* (2006), available at: http://www.pewinternet.org/Reports/2006/Online-Dating.aspx. Online relationships formation statistics from M. Rosenfeld, "Searching for a Mate: The Rise of the Internet as a Social Intermediary," *American Sociological Review* 77 (2012): 523–547.

3. See the following surveys of online relationships: Nick Yee, "The Demographics, Motivations and Derived Experiences of Users of Massively-Multiuser Online Graphical Environments," *Presence* 15 (2006): 309–329; Nick Yee, "Love Is in the Air," *The Daedalus Project* (2006): http://www.nickyee.com/daedalus/archives /001528.php; and Helena Cole and Mark D. Griffiths, "Social Interactions in Massively Multiplayer Online Role-Playing Games," *CyberPsychology and Behavior* 10 (2007): 575–583.

4. Some guilds span multiple online games, and members can thus remain in the same guild even when they're playing a different game.

5. Todd Krieger, "Love and Money," *Wired*, March 9, 1995.

6. See Russ V. Reynolds, J. Regis McNamara, Richard J. Marion, and David L. Tobin, "Computerized Service Delivery in Clinical Psychology," *Professional Psychology: Research and Practice* 16 (1985): 339–353; Malcolm R. Parks and Kory Floyd, "Making Friends in Cyberspace," *Journal of Communication* 46 (1996): 80–97; Yee, "Demographics, Motivations and Derived Experiences"; and Joseph B. Walther, "Computer-Mediated Communication: Impersonal, Interpersonal, and Hyperpersonal Interaction," *Communication Research* 23 (1996): 3–43.

7. Susan M. Wildermuth and Sally Vogl-Bauer, "We Met on the Net: Exploring the Perceptions of Online Romantic Relationships Participants," *Southern Communication Journal* 72 (2007): 211–227.

8. Katelyn Y. A. McKenna and John A. Bargh, "Plan 9 from Cyberspace: The Implications of the Internet for Personality and Social Psychology," *Personality and Social Psychology Review* 4 (2000): 57–75.

9. Mark Seal, *The Man in the Rockefeller Suit: The Astonishing Rise and Spectacular Fall of a Serial Impostor* (New York: Viking Adult, 2011).

10. Bruno Bettelheim, *The Uses of Enchantment: The Meaning and Importance of Fairy Tales* (New York: Alfred A. Knopf, 1975), 69.

11. Eli J. Finkel et al., "Online Dating: A Critical Analysis from the Perspective of Psychological Science," *Psychological Science in the Public Interest* 13 (2012): 3–66.

Chapter Eight. **Tools of Persuasion and Control**

1. Linden Labs, "Factsheet: The Technology behind the Second Life Platform," http://lindenlab.com/pressroom/general/factsheets/technology.

2. Charles A. Nelson, "The Development and Neural Bases of Face Recognition," *Infant and Child Development* 10 (2001): 3–18. See also Carolyn C. Goren, Merrill Sarty, and Paul Y. K. Wu, "Visual Following and Pattern Discrimination of Face-Like Stimuli by Newborn Infants," *Pediatrics* 56 (1975): 544–549.

3. Ellen Berscheid and Elaine Hatfield Walster, *Interpersonal Attraction* (Menlo Park, CA: Addison-Wesley, 1979). Also see James Shanteau and Geraldine F. Nagy, "Probability of Acceptance in Dating Choice," *Journal of Personality and Social Psychology* 37 (1979): 522–533.

4. Jerry M. Burger et al., "What a Coincidence! The Effects of Incidental Similarity on Compliance," *Personality and Social Psychology Bulletin* 30 (2004): 35–43.

5. See Experiment 2 reported in Jeremy N. Bailenson, Shanto Iyengar, Nick Yee, and Nathan A. Collins, "Facial Similarity between Voters and Candidates Causes Influence," *Public Opinion Quarterly* 72 (2008): 935–961.

6. Our first study used undergraduate students and less well known political candidates: Jeremy N. Bailenson, Philip Garland, Shanto Iyengar, and Nick Yee, "Transformed Facial Similarity as a Political Cue: A Preliminary Investigation," *Political Science* 27 (2006): 373–386. Then we followed up with three studies using nationally representative voting-age US citizens in Bailenson, Iyengar, Yee, and Collins, "Facial Similarity between Voters and Candidates."

7. Jeremy N. Bailenson et al., "The Use of Immersive Virtual Reality in the Learning Science: Digital Transformations of Teachers, Students, and Social Context," *Journal of the Learning Science* 17 (2008): 102–141.

8. Valins's bogus heartbeat study is reported in Stuart Valins, "Cognitive Effects of False Heart-Rate Feedback," *Journal of Personality and Social Psychology* 4 (1966): 400–408. For the original formulation of self-perception theory, see Daryl J. Bem, "Self-Perception Theory," in *Advances in Experimental Social Psychology*, vol. 6, ed. Leonard Berkowitz (New York: Academic Press, 1972), 1–62.

9. Donald G. Dutton and Arthur P. Aron, "Some Evidence for Heightened Sexual Attraction under Conditions of High Anxiety," *Journal of Personality and Social Psychology* 30 (1974): 510–517.

10. Mark G. Frank and Thomas Gilovich, "The Dark Side of Self and Social Perception: Black Uniforms and Aggression in Professional Sports," *Journal of Personality and Social Psychology* 54 (1988): 74–85.

11. The seminal paper linking attractiveness with positive perceptions is Karen Dion, Ellen Berscheid, and Elaine Walster, "What Is Beautiful Is Good," *Journal of Personality and Social Psychology* 24 (1972): 285–290. The large meta-analytic review of hundreds of papers on attractiveness is reported in Judith H. Langlois et al., "Maxims

or Myths of Beauty? A Meta-Analytic and Theoretical Review," *Psychological Bulletin* 126 (2000): 390–423. The jury sentencing example comes from Harold Sigall and Nancy Ostrove, "Beautiful but Dangerous: Effects of Offender Attractiveness and Nature of the Crime on Juridic Judgment," *Journal of Personality and Social Psychology* 31 (1975): 410–414.

12. See study one in Nick Yee and Jeremy N. Bailenson, "The Proteus Effect: The Effect of Transformed Self-Representation on Behavior," *Human Communication Research* 33 (2007): 271–290.

13. For an example of a study that links height with perceived competence, see Thomas J. Young and Laurence A. French, "Height and Perceived Competence of U.S. Presidents," *Perceptual and Motor Skills* 82 (1996): 1002. The large-sample regression model of the impact of height on income is reported in Timothy A. Judge and Daniel M. Cable, "The Effect of Physical Height on Workplace Success and Income: Preliminary Test of a Theoretical Model," *Journal of Applied Psychology* 89 (2004): 428–441. The exact estimated impact of each inch of increase in height on annual earning is $789 (435).

14. See study two in Yee and Bailenson, "Proteus Effect."

15. Nick Yee, Jeremy N. Bailenson, and Nicolas Ducheneaut, "The Proteus Effect: Implications of Transformed Digital Self-Representation on Online and Offline Behavior," *Communication Research* 36 (2009): 285–312.

16. For retirement savings estimates, see Diana Ferrell et al., *Talkin' 'bout My Generation: The Economic Impact of Aging US Baby Boomers* (McKinsey Global Institute, 2008); and Ruth Helman et al., *The 2012 Retirement Confidence Survey: Job Insecurity, Debt Weigh on Retirement Confidence, Savings* (Employee Benefit Research Institute, 2012).

17. Hal E. Hershfield et al., "Increasing Saving Behavior through Age-Progressed Renderings of the Future Self," *Journal of Marketing Research* 48 (2011): S23–S37.

18. Jesse Fox and Jeremy N. Bailenson, "Virtual Self-Modeling: The Effects of Vicarious Reinforcement and Identification on Exercise Behaviors," *Media Psychology* 12 (2009): 1–25.

Chapter Nine. Introverted Elves, Conscientious Gnomes, and the Quest for Big Data

1. The four papers generated from the early PlayOn data were Nicolas Ducheneaut, Nick Yee, Eric Nickell, and Robert Moore, "Alone Together? Exploring the Social Dynamics of Massively Multiplayer Games," *Proceedings of CHI 2006* (2006): 407–416; Nicolas Ducheneaut, Nick Yee, Eric Nickell, and Robert Moore, "Building an MMO with Mass Appeal: A Look at Gameplay in World of Warcraft," *Games and Culture* 1 (2006): 281–317; Dmitri Williams et al., "From Tree House to Barracks: The Social Life of Guilds in World of Warcraft," *Games and Culture* 1 (2006): 338–361; and Nicolas Ducheneaut, Nick Yee, Eric Nickell, and Robert Moore, "The Life and Death

of Online Gaming Communities: A Look at Guilds in World of Warcraft," *Proceedings of CHI 2007* (2007): 839–848.

2. See John P. Robinson, Phillip R. Shaver, and Lawrence S. Wrightsman, *Measures of Personality and Social Psychological Attitudes*, vol. 1: *Measures of Social Psychological Attitudes* (New York: Academic Press, 1991); and Oliver P. John and Sanjay Srivastava, "The Big Five Trait Taxonomy: History, Measurement, and Theoretical Perspectives," *Handbook of Personality: Theory and Research*, ed. Lawrence A. Pervin and Oliver P. John (New York: Guilford, 1999), 102–138. See also Lewis R. Goldberg, "A Historical Survey of Personality Scales and Inventories," in *Advances in Psychological Assessment*, vol. 1, ed. Paul McReynolds (Palo Alto, CA: Science and Behavior Books, 1975), 293–336.

3. See John and Srivastava, "Big Five Trait Taxonomy," for a wonderful historical and conceptual overview of Big Five development. For all that the Big Five model has done to unify the field and advance personality research, it's still important to acknowledge its weaknesses. See, e.g., Jack Block, "The Five-Factor Framing of Personality and Beyond: Some Ruminations," *Psychological Inquiry* 21 (2010): 2–25. In particular, certain traits that are well captured in the English language are not in the Big Five, including honesty, masculinity-femininity, humor or wit, and sensuality.

4. For earlier studies involving personality assessment among strangers, see David C. Funder and Carl D. Sneed, "Behavioral Manifestations of Personality: An Ecological Approach to Judgmental Accuracy," *Journal of Personality and Social Psychology* 64 (1993): 479–490; and David A. Kenny, Caryl Horner, Deborah A. Kashy, and Ling-chuan Chu, "Consensus at Zero Acquaintance: Replication, Behavioral Cues, and Stability," *Journal of Personality and Social Psychology* 62 (1992): 88–97. The study on personality expression in bedrooms and offices is reported in Samuel D. Gosling, Sei Jin Ko, Thomas Mannarelli, and Margaret E. Morris, "A Room with a Cue: Judgments of Personality Based on Offices and Bedrooms," *Journal of Personality and Social Psychology* 82 (2002): 379–398.

5. For personal websites, see Simine Vazire and Samuel D. Gosling, "e-Perceptions: Personality Impressions Based on Personal Websites," *Journal of Personality and Social Psychology* 87 (2004): 123–132. For Facebook profiles, see Mitja D. Back et al., "Facebook Profiles Reflect Actual Personality, not Self-Idealization," *Psychological Science* 21 (2010): 372–374. For email content, see Alastair J. Gill, Jon Oberlander, and Elizabeth Austin, "Rating E-Mail Personality at Zero Acquaintance," *Personality and Individual Differences* 40 (2006): 497–507. For email addresses, see Mitja D. Back, Stefan C. Schmukle, and Boris Egloff, "How Extraverted Is honey.bunny77@ hotmail.de? Inferring Personality from E-Mail Addresses," *Journal of Research in Personality* 42 (2008): 1116–1122.

6. Dmitry Nozhnin, "Predicting Churn: Data-Mining Your Game," *Gama Sutra*, May 17, 2012, http://www.gamasutra.com/view/feature /170472/predicting_churn_datamining_your_.php.

7. Nick Yee, Nicolas Ducheneaut, Les Nelson, and Peter Likarish, "Introverted Elves and Conscientious Gnomes: The Expression of Personality in World of Warcraft," *Proceedings of CHI 2011* (2011): 753–762.

8. Charles Duhigg, "How Companies Learn Your Secrets," *New York Times*, February 16, 2012.

9. Machine learning analysis of this data set was reported in Peter Likarish et al., "Demographic Profiling from MMOG Gameplay" (Paper presented at the Privacy Enhancing Technologies Symposium, 2011). The specific rules we list here in the book chapter were not reported in that paper. These rules were derived using an association rule mining algorithm in the Weka toolkit called HotSpot. Peter Steiner's well-known cartoon was published in the *New Yorker* on July 5, 1993. The indoor gardening story is reported in Heather Hollingsworth, "Kansas Couple: Indoor Gardening Prompted Pot Raid," *Associated Press*, March 29, 2013.

10. For more on the "digital enclosure," see Mark Andrejevic, "Surveillance in the Digital Enclosure," *Communication Review* 10 (2007): 295–317. Screenshots of the Naked Gnome Protest, along with the account suspension message, can be found at: http://www.cesspit.net/drupal/node/491.

Chapter Ten. **Changing the Rules**

Epigraph: Lawrence Lessig, *Code* (New York: Basic Books, 1999), 58–59.

1. The wallet-dropping experiments are reported in Mark D. West, "Losers: Recovering Lost Property in Japan and the United States," Michigan Law and Economics Research Paper No. 02-005 (2002), available at SSRN: http://ssrn.com/abstract=316119. Tsunamic recovery statistics reported in Tom Miyagawa Coulton and John M. Glionna, "Japanese Return Cash Recovered after Tsunami," *Los Angeles Times*, September 22, 2011.

2. Walter Mischel, *Personality and Assessment* (New York: Wiley, 1968). For an interactionist approach, see Allan R. Buss, "The Trait-Situation Controversy and the Concept of Interaction," *Personality and Social Psychology Bulletin* 3 (1977): 196–201.

3. Nick Yee, "Time Spent in the Meta-Game," *The Daedalus Project* (2006).

4. Nicolas Ducheneaut, Nick Yee, Eric Nickell, and Robert J. Moore, " 'Alone Together?' Exploring the Social Dynamics of Massively Multiplayer Games," *Proceedings of CHI* 1 (2006): 407–416.

5. Sherry Turkle, *Alone Together: Why We Expect More from Technology and Less from Each Other* (New York: Basic Books, 2011), 19.

Chapter Eleven. **The Hidden Logic of Avatars**

1. See Jim Blascovich and Jeremy Bailenson, *Infinite Reality: The Hidden Blueprint of Our Virtual Lives* (New York: HarperCollins, 2011), for the historical background of and current research in virtual reality.

2. Barlow's documentation of his virtual reality experience can be found in John Perry Barlow, *Being in Nothingness: Virtual Reality and the Pioneers of Cyberspace* (n.d.), available from: http://w2.eff.org/Misc/Publications/John_Perry_Barlow/HTML/ being_in_nothingness.html. The counterculture's fascination with technology is documented in Tom Wolfe, *The Electric Kool-Aid Acid Test* (New York: Farrar, Straus and Giroux, 1973). For a fascinating account of how the counterculture gave rise to personal computing, see Fred Turner, *From Counterculture to Cyberculture: Stewart Brand, the Whole Earth Network, and the Rise of Digital Utopianism* (Chicago: University of Chicago Press, 2006).

3. William Swartout et al., "Simulation Meets Hollywood: Integrating Graphics, Sound, Story and Character for Immersive Simulation," *Multimodal Intelligent Information Presentation Series: Text, Speech and Language Technology* 27 (2005): 297–303.

4. Byron Reeves and J. Leighton Read, *Total Engagement: Using Games and Virtual Worlds to Change the Way People Work and Businesses Compete* (Boston: Harvard Business School, 2009).

5. Philip Rosedale, "Second Life: What Do We Learn If We Digitize Everything?" (Paper presented at the Long Now Foundation, San Francisco, November 30, 2006, video of the talk available at: http://longnow.org/seminars/02006/). For the schizophrenia simulation in *Second Life*, see Jane Elliott, "What's It Like to Have Schizophrenia?" *BBC News*, March 19, 2007, available at: http://news.bbc.co.uk/2 /hi/health/6453241.stm.

6. Pavel Curtis and David A. Nichols, "MUDs Grow Up: Social Virtual Reality in the Real World," *Xerox PARC*, January 19, 1993, available at: http://w2.eff.org / Net_culture/MOO_MUD_IRC/muds_grow_up.paper.

7. Julian Dibbell, "A Rape in Cyberspace," *Village Voice*, December 23, 1993.

8. Jaron Lanier, *You Are Not a Gadget* (New York: Vintage, 2011), 10.

9. Raph Koster, *MUD Influence*, June 27, 2008, at: http://www.raphkoster.com /2008/06/27/mud-influence/.

10. Jaron Lanier, "Homuncular Flexibility," *Edge*, January 1, 2006, available at: http://www.edge.org/q2006/q06_print.html#lanier.

Chapter Twelve. **Reflections and the Future of Virtual Worlds**

1. See Eric T. Lofgren and Nina H. Fefferman, "The Untapped Potential of Virtual Game Worlds to Shed Light on Real World Epidemics," *Lancet Infectious Diseases* 7 (2007): 625–629; and Edward Castronova, "Virtual Worlds: Petri Dishes, Rat Mazes, and Supercolliders," *Games and Culture* 4 (2009): 396–407.

2. Jon A. Krosnick, Joanne M. Miller, and Michael P. Tichy, "An Unrecognized Need for Ballot Reform: Effects of Candidate Name Order," in *Rethinking the Vote: The Politics and Prospects of American Election Reform*, ed. Ann N. Crigler, Marion R. Just, and Edward J. McCaffery (New York: Oxford University Press, 2004), 51–74.

3. Lisa Nakamura, *Cybertypes: Race, Ethnicity, and Identity on the Internet* (New York: Routledge, 2002).

4. For more on the connections between the military and the entertainment industry, see Tim Lenoir and Henry Lowood, "Theatres of War: The Military-Entertainment Complex," in *Kunstkammer, Laboratorium, Bühne—Schauplätze des Wissens im 17. Jahrhundert*, ed. Jan Lazardig, Helmar Schramm, and Ludger Scharte (Berlin: Walter de Gruyter, 2003).

GLOSSARY OF ONLINE GAMING TERMS

This glossary covers online game terminology that appears in this book. For a more comprehensive glossary, please refer to: http://www.nickyee.com/daedalus/archives/001313.php.

Add. Noun. Short for *additional.* Refers to an additional mob that unexpectedly appears (and thus must be dealt with) during a fight.

Aggro. Verb/Noun. Short for *aggression.* As a noun, *aggro* refers to the amount of hostility the player has generated on a mob by damaging it. In turn, mobs attack the character that is highest on its *aggro* list. As a verb, *aggro* refers to drawing a mob's attention, either intentionally or accidentally.

Alt. See *Alternate.*

Alternate. Adjective/Noun. Refers to an *alternate* character a player has apart from his or her main character. Commonly abbreviated to *alt.* This is a fluid and personal categorization that varies from player to player. Sometimes players get tired of their main and spend more time on their *alt.*

Bind. Verb/Noun. In certain online games, characters are teleported back to a designated safe spot when they die. The act of designating a spot is called *binding.* In some games, characters can *bind* themselves. In other games, they must interact with a specific NPC or ask characters of a specific class to *bind* them.

Boss. Noun. Usually short for a *boss monster,* a challenging mob at strategic points in a dungeon or raid.

Bot. Noun/Verb. Short for *robot.* Refers to automated scripts that play the game for a character using simulated mouse and keyboard commands. This practice is often explicitly banned in games and can lead to termination of the account if uncovered by the game developers.

Buff. Noun/Verb. A spell that temporarily boosts a character's abilities or attributes. In verb form, *buff* refers to the act of casting this spell.

Camp. Verb. To wait in an area to hunt one or more specific mobs. Can be used negatively to imply the selfish hoarding of a mob or an area.

Class. Noun. Refers to combat professions in online games and role-playing games. Examples include warrior, cleric, druid, and necromancer.

Corpse. Noun. In some online games, a *corpse* appears where the player has died. Sometimes all the player's items and money are left on the *corpse* and the player is teleported back to his or her bind spot. *Corpses* typically decay after a certain time proportional to the character's level.

Corpse Run. Noun. The act of retrieving your corpse after you have died. This is typically a perilous task because people tend to die in dangerous places rather than safe places.

Crafting. Adjective/Noun. A general category of skills that allow players to create usable objects and equipment from raw resources. Examples include tailoring, blacksmithing, and cooking.

Crit. See *Critical*.

Critical. Adjective/Verb/Noun. When dealing damage with spells or weapons, characters have a low probability of landing a particularly heavy blow, referred to as a *critical hit*, *critical* for short, and often abbreviated as *crit*. A crit often deals 50 percent or more damage than usual.

DPS. Noun. Short for *Damage Per Second*. In the context of combat statistics, DPS refers to the mathematical calculation of damage dealt by a character per second. Thus, a character with higher DPS can inflict more damage over time than a character with low DPS. In the context of combat classes, DPS refers to classes that deal high DPS and is one of the three combat archetypes in online games. See also *Healer* and *Tank*.

Drop. Verb/Noun. Refers to a specific item that a mob may provide as treasure when killed. In this usage, *drop* can be thought of as one specific item among a mob's loot—the sum of its *drops*. As a verb, *drop* refers to the act of a mob providing loot when it dies.

Dungeon. Noun. A series of passages and rooms with mobs and bosses in an online game. These are not necessarily underground, although many are. See also *Instance*.

Experience. Noun. Characters need to accumulate *experience* points to level up. Experience can be gained by killing mobs, completing quests, and accomplishing other in-game objectives.

Farm. Verb. To kill a mob repeatedly to accumulate or find a specific drop. Often used in the same context as camping (see *Camp*).

Gold Farming. The act of accumulating in-game currency to sell for real-world currency. A player who is suspected of or confirmed to be accumulating in-game currency to sell for real-world currency is called a *Gold Farmer*. These labels are often used pejoratively.

Guild. Noun. A long-term player organization that can range in size from one to more than two hundred players. Players often have to pay a small fee to start a *guild*. They can then name the *guild* and recruit other players to it. In online games, *guilds* facilitate larger dungeon and raid encounters. They also enable sustained social interaction among a group of players.

Healer. Noun. Combat class that focuses on restoring the health of team members during fights. One of three combat archetypes. See also *DPS* and *Tank*.

Instance. Noun. One of many parallel versions of an area, usually a dungeon, in an online game. To avoid overcrowding in dungeons, each player group entering a dungeon receives its own version of it, termed an *instance* of that dungeon. This usage of *instance* is a reference to object-oriented programming. In contemporary online games, *instance* is often synonymous with *Dungeon*.

Loot. Noun / Verb. As a noun, *loot* refers to the collection of items and in-game currency that a mob drops when it dies. As a verb, *loot* refers to the act of gathering items and in-game currency from a dead mob. See also *Drop*.

Mana. Noun. A resource that magic users draw from to cast spells. Players use *mana* to cast spells, after which their *mana* recovers slowly over time.

MMO. Often used as the abbreviated form of MMORPG, although it can also be used as a more inclusive category of all persistent online games that can support many players at once.

MMORPG. Short for *Massively Multiplayer Online Role-Playing Game*. Often abbreviated to MMO or MMOG.

Mob. Noun. Short for *mobile*, a coin termed in MUD by Richard Bartle to refer to computer-controlled monsters that would move around the map on their own.

Mod. Noun / Verb. Short for *modify* or *modification*. In a gaming context, a *mod* is a third-party-created piece of software that extends an existing game in some way. For example, a player might create new textures for the existing 3D models. To *mod* a game is to create this additional functionality. Different games have varying rules in terms of whether *modding* is allowed and in what contexts. Most online games do not allow *modding*.

MUD. Short for *Multi-User Dungeon*, or text-based multiplayer online world, created in the late 1970s. The predecessor of online games.

Nerf. Noun/Verb. As a verb, the actions taken by game developers to reduce a character class or race's abilities in order to balance an online game. Owing to the complex rules of and interactions in online games, it is often difficult for game developers to ensure that every character class performs equally well in combat throughout the game's content. When imbalances are noticed, developers may bring certain abilities in line with the average. This almost always has the effect of upsetting players who were playing those classes or races. As a noun, a *nerf* refers to the specific rule change that reduces a certain ability.

Newbie. Noun. A new player.

Ninja. Verb. As a verb, to purposely loot a drop off a monster by disregarding the agreed-upon rules of the group—in a sense, stealing the item. Depending on the game, this can occur in different ways. In *World of Warcraft*, it was possible at one point for a player to roll on an item that he or she could not use. A *ninja* might exploit this mechanism to attempt to win a roll this way. Players who *ninja* an item are referred to as *ninja looters*. See also *Roll*.

Noob. Noun. The pejorative form of *Newbie*.

NPC. Short for *Non-Player Character*. A character controlled by the computer.

Patrol. Noun. A mob that has a set, looping path. In a dungeon, it is important to be aware of *patrols* and their spawning intervals. Abbreviated to *Pat*.

Pull. Verb. To initiate combat with one or more monsters by luring it toward the group. In most dungeons, the group will stay at a safe location while one character, the *puller*, lures monsters toward the group.

PvE. Adjective. Short for *Player Versus Environment*. In this context, environment refers to monsters controlled by the computer. In other words, you cannot be killed by other players except under mutually consensual conditions.

PvP. Adjective. Short for *Player Versus Player*. In other words, players may freely kill each other outside a few safe areas.

Race. Noun. In the context of online games, *race* refers to fantastical creatures. Examples include Elves, Trolls, and Gnomes.

Raid. Noun/Verb. As a noun, *raid* refers to a challenging dungeon for a normal or large group of players. In *World of Warcraft*, some *raids* require up to twenty-five players. *Raids* involve more challenging mobs, bosses, and tactics than normal dungeons and may require many hours to complete. In *World of Warcraft*, a group may attempt to complete a *raid* over a one-week period if it cannot complete it in one run. As a verb, *raiding* refers to an attempt at completing a high-level dungeon.

Rez. Noun / Verb. Short for *resurrection* or *resurrect*. As a verb, the act of using a spell or ability to return a dead player to life. As a noun, *rez* refers to the actual spell or ability.

RL. Short for *Real Life*.

Roll. Noun / Verb. As a verb, the act of using the in-game random number generator to decide which character should receive the loot. Thus, each character *rolls* a virtual hundred-sided die, and the character with the highest result wins the loot. As a noun, *roll* refers to the actual random outcome.

RW. Short for *Real World*.

Server. Noun. For technical reasons, it is often difficult to maintain a stable online world with thousands of players. Most online games thus split the game population into parallel universes, each on its own *server*. When players start playing an online game, they select a *server* to join and their character lives specifically on that *server*.

Shard. Noun. Synonymous with *server*. Originally used to refer to servers in *Ultima Online*.

Solo. Verb. The act of playing an online game alone. More specifically, the act of being able to kill mobs that are the same or even higher level than the character with relative ease and safety. In online games, certain classes are designed to be able to *solo* well while others are more dependent on groups.

Spawn. Verb. In reference to a mob, to reappear after being killed. In most online games, mobs *respawn* after a set interval, as in, "He's waiting for the goblin chieftain to *spawn*."

Spec. Noun / Verb. Short for *specialization*. In online games, each character class's abilities and skills can be configured in many ways. Each combination is referred to as a *specialization*, or *spec* for short. Although there are many configurations, optimal configurations are described by their intended goals. For example, a druid may have both a healing *spec* and a DPS *spec*.

Tank. Noun / Verb. As a noun, one of the combat archetypes. A *tank* is a durable character who shields the group from the brunt of the enemy's attacks by standing in front and taunting the enemies. As a verb, it means taking on this role in a fight.

Wipe. Noun / Verb. As a verb, in reference to a group, to be completely overwhelmed and killed by mobs or a boss, generally in difficult dungeons or raids. As a noun, a *wipe* is a specific instance of this happening.

XP. Noun. Abbreviation of *Experience*.

Zone. Verb / Noun. As a noun, a bounded geographical area in an online game. As a verb, the act of crossing a geographical boundary in a game.

INDEX